INSPIRE!

Cover design by OpalWorks Pte Ltd

An imprint of Marshall Cavendish International

PO Box 65829
London EC1P 1NY
United Kingdom
info@marshallcavendish.co.uk

and

1 New Industrial Road
Singapore 536196
genrefsales@sg.marshallcavendish.com
www.marshallcavendish.com/genref

Marshall Cavendish is a trademark of Times Publishing Limited

Other Marshall Cavendish offices:
Marshall Cavendish International (Asia) Private Limited, 1 New Industrial Road, Singapore 536196 • Marshall Cavendish Corporation, 99 White Plains Road, Tarrytown NY 10591–9001, USA • Marshall Cavendish International (Thailand) Co Ltd, 253 Asoke, 12th Floor, Sukhumvit 21 Road, Klongtoey Nua, Wattana, Bangkok 10110, Thailand • Marshall Cavendish (Malaysia) Sdn Bhd, Times Subang, Lot 46, Subang Hi-Tech Industrial Park, Batu Tiga, 40000 Shah Alam, Selangor Darul Ehsan, Malaysia

A CIP record for this book is available from the British Library

ISBN 978-981-4302-62-3

Printed and bound in the United Kingdom by CPI Mackays, Chatham ME5 8TD

SIMON MAIER

INSPIRE!

INSIGHTS AND LESSONS

from

100 OF THE GREATEST SPEECHES

from

FILM AND THEATRE

Marshall Cavendish
Business

FOR JANE

"I have met with women who I really think would like to be married to a poem, and to be given away by a novel." John Keats

"According to an opinion poll, 13 per cent of women in the United States cannot say whether they wear their tights under their knickers or over them. That's something like a million women walking around in a state of chronic foundation garment uncertainty." Bill Bryson, *Notes from a Big Country*

"I can no other answer make but thanks,
And thanks; and ever thanks..." William Shakespeare, *Twelfth Night*

CONTENTS

INTRODUCTION

"Stand up. Your father's passing." Reverend Sykes (William Walker) to Scout (Mary Badham) as her father Atticus Finch (Gregory Peck) exits the court after having just lost the case defending Tom Robinson (Brock Peters) in the film *To Kill a Mockingbird* (1962)

Mark Twain is alleged to have said, "Twenty years from now, you will be more disappointed by the things you did not do than by the things you did do. So, throw off the bowlines. Sail away from the safe harbor. Catch the trade winds in your sails. Explore. Dream. Discover." Whoever actually said this was right. This is a tacit instruction to let the imagination soar, to let inspiration take hold. We are all inspired by some aspect of the world around us, some small or vast thing we see, perhaps some dot in our imagination that pushes us beyond pondering. All of us, in one way or another, are moved, delighted or distressed by a variety of things that bump an emotion. Not all of us are affected by the same things of course, but there are some that touch most of us in certain and often similar ways. Besides those things we witness every day that inspire us – a child, bravery, a smile – there are scenes in plays or films that inspire us or prompt an emotional response.

And this, of course, is where it gets messy and, in truth, this book should stop right now because we enter tricky territory for the field of exploring human emotion is complex and varied. It's dangerous to generalise – yet generalise we must in this book. Some emotions are manifest by obvious signs of enjoyment, elation, anger, distress or terror. In some cases, our emotions seem to be a blend of different states.

Most of us relish the emotions that are displayed in movies and theatre. That's part of their appeal. Plays and films provide a mirror on life – sometimes inspirational examples of the lives of others that allow us to feel emotions quite openly and in moderate safety. There are moments when some of us weep, laugh, smile, frown, hate or feel proud, others when we get a tingle down our spine, yet others where we clench our fists or grind our teeth – because, for example, we know what the hero doesn't. It's the Othello moment. There are times where we gasp at the sheer horror of an action or in absolute disgust at another. We marvel at the goodness or selflessness of a hero, shout "yippee" in our heads when the bad guys get their just desserts, or feel indignant when they don't.

Some of the most unforgettable speeches and uplifting moments come from movies and theatre because these art forms express uplift and emotion. Film and theatrical speeches or moments don't have to be long to be good. Sometimes one or two sentences will do it. They stick in our memories and enhance all sorts of situations – legal, political, social, commercial. Phrases such as "Once more unto the breech ..." have become iconic. This isn't surprising really because they are easily transportable to other contexts – real life contexts – where they reinforce feelings and emotions. They express what we sometimes find hard to put into words. Other phrases contextulise stories and plots that we enjoy and help us understand (or at least rationalise) the real world. Since time immemorial, stories have been the way of defining the immediate world, contextualising the past, appraising the future and teaching us caution, values and moral integrity. Speeches that recall a good story paint a picture in our minds that helps us recall life's moments and points in our histories at which we cried or laughed.

There are only so many storylines that exist in any culture. Many stories have commonalities and the underlying structures of all stories anywhere are similar. The plotlines are basic. For example, one is what might be called "beating the wicked monster", where the all-powerful, terrifying monster has existed for years threatening and (probably) devouring the locals. Nothing can be done until a hero or heroine arrives to destroy the dreadful monster. This may seem to be a genre just for children, but it really isn't. Grown up examples are *The Silence of the Lambs* film (1991) and book of the same name by Thomas Harris (1981), the great novel *Dracula (*1897) by Bram Stoker, the Old English heroic poem *Beowulf*, and, of course, for both children and adults, the English fairy tales *Jack and the Beanstalk (*originally by Benjamin Tabart in 1807) and *Hansel and Gretel* (by the Grimm Brothers in 1812).

Then there is the "rags to riches" storyline where the central character is taken from an ordinary environment to huge power, greatness or wealth. An alternative angle here might be where the hero, who seemingly lives a humdrum life, actually hides another exceptional heroic side to his character that is only exposed in times of duress (a bit like Clark Kent). Another version is where the power or riches are removed from the hero and only returned once something or someone dark or evil is defeated. Examples include *Les Misérables*, both a book by Victor Hugo (1862) and an award-winning musical (1980), the Arabian Nights story *Aladdin* (1706), *Cinderella* (the 1697 "modern" version by Charles Perrault), Charlotte Brontë's *Jane Eyre* (1847), along with most superheroes.

"The long arduous search, quest or mission" storyline is one that resonates back into the mists of time. Here a hero finds out about a goal or prize that no one to date has ever been able to manage or capture. Whatever the reason for the hero to undertake the quest (perhaps with marriage to a prince or princess as the prize, or the possibility of vast treasure, or even immortality), the journey is always hazardous and difficult. Examples are *The Odyssey* (attributed to Homer), *The Count of Monte Cristo* by Alexandre Dumas (1844), the *Raiders of the Lost Ark* franchise (first movie in 1981) and *The Shawshank Redemption* movie (1994). Actually, most of the Eastwood spaghetti Westerns could be said to follow this pattern. And there's *The Wizard of Oz* (1939) based on the 1900 children's novel *The Wonderful Wizard of Oz* by L. Frank Baum, and *The Lord of the Rings* movie trilogy

(2001–03) from the J. R. R. Tolkein book of the same name (1954–55). Sometimes the hero has no desire to return home after the quest because the prize at the end of it is perfect. Sir Galahad's Arthurian quest for the Holy Grail is to find it, *not* return with it.

However, some stories regard the returning *and* the coming back as important. We all like stories of people travelling, having great adventures and definitely returning. While the experience is initially wonderful and awe-inspiring, there is a sense of increasing foreboding, danger and eventually some disaster before the sweet lights of home are seen again. Some of the tales already mentioned might come into this genre; others would include Jules Verne's *Journey to the Centre of the Earth* (1864) and *Alice's Adventures in Wonderland (*1865), a story by Charles Dodgson (Lewis Carroll). Then there's the film *Back to the Future (*1985) plus the franchise that followed, and *Gulliver's Travels* by Jonathan Swift (1726).

The word "comedy" is hard to define properly sometimes. Comedy is actually a difficult genre because many other genres dip into it and it into them. Usually a comedy follows a hapless hero or heroine along a path of misunderstandings and some chaos until all the strands and subplots become clear. The endings are usually happy and the problems solved. Shakespeare's comedies come to mind where there's usually a struggle of young lovers to overcome some difficulty or problem, the cause of which is usually older folk in one of the families. Examples would include *Much Ado About Nothing, Midsummer Night's Dream, As You Like It* and *The Merry Wives of Windsor.* And from the world of movies, there is, for instance, *Some Like It Hot* (1959), *The Pink Panther* (1964), *Annie Hall* (1977) and *Groundhog Day* (1993). In the world of theatre we can include the likes of William Wycherley's wonderful *The Country Wife* (1675), Oliver Goldsmith's *She Stoops to Conquer* (1773) and Oscar Wilde's *The Importance of Being Earnest* (1895). In modern times, comedy relates to anything that's regarded as funny and covers a great deal of ground. Aristotle described comedy as showing people to be worse than they are, and tragedy as showing people to be greater than they are. That's not how it works now. Most people would say a comedic story is where all the characters are thrown into a state of bewilderment, misunderstanding, stupidity or darkness – and resolution can only come when these constricting factors have been played out to their extremes. Comedy, of course, can inspire as much as any other type of story.

Another plot approach involves an element of tragedy where a lead character has some flaw in his or her personality, or who is in the wrong place at the wrong time, or does a bad or very wrong thing – the consequences of which are huge. He or she is drawn towards a terrible course of action which results in disaster or ruin. In many Greek tragedies, the central character is an individual (usually a prince, king or queen) who goes through a series of actions and decisions that unwittingly brings about his or her own downfall. The story of Oedipus is a good example and that line is followed in many tragic stories down the ages. Broad examples include Flaubert's *Madame Bovary* (1857), Oscar Wilde's *The Picture of Dorian Gray* (1890) and the movie *Bonnie and Clyde* (1967); and of course Shakespeare's *Antony and Cleopatra, King Lear, Hamlet, Julius Caesar, Macbeth, Othello* and *Romeo and Juliet*. Most of Ibsen's plays are tragic, as is, for example, *Wuthering Heights* (1847) by Emily Bronte.

The process of finding oneself (or the notion of rebirth) is another storyline. What generally happens here is that the hero or heroine is oppressed by some dark force or influence until he or she has become a different person. A slightly alternative take on this theme is that the protagonist is often cast under some dark spell either instigated by himself or herself or, more likely, by an outside force. Whichever the approach, the hero/heroine is gripped by a terrible, dark power. When it seems that the dark power has triumphed, a reversal takes place and the hero is redeemed somehow – usually through a love interest and hope. Many fairy tales take this form, as do classic tales like *A Christmas Carol* (1843) by Charles Dickens, the George Eliot novel *Silas Marner* (1861) and the film *It's a Wonderful Life* (1946). Usually, but not always, any tragic story has resolution and concludes with "happily ever after" – something sought by adults as much as by children. We find resolution inspirational.

What actually makes a good film or play is highly subjective, of course. It's not just down to the piece that wins an Oscar, BAFTA or an Olivier. It's a mix of story, plot and script, music, photography in a movie and, of course, acting. It's also about taste and what presses your particular buttons.

And from films and plays, we have many of the most famous speeches ever delivered. The stark, matter-of-fact presentation by George C. Scott of the speech by General George S. Patton to his troops in the film *Patton* (1970) defined the purpose of a generation in its battle against tyranny and fear. His admonition that you don't become a hero by dying for your country, but by making someone else die for theirs, painted a grim picture of the realities of war, even if you don't agree with his precept. Finding the courage to continue against seemingly insurmountable odds is the focus of the speech by England's King Henry V from two films based on and including the Shakespeare play, *Henry V.* Speeches from the play have been used many times to inspire in times of war, by politicians in times of trouble and by business leaders in times of need.

In a similar vein is the short speech given by Aragorn in the third of *The Lord of the Rings* franchise, *The Return of the King* (2003), when leading his armies of men against the forces of the Dark Lord Sauron. Aragorn pledges to his men that, "a day may come when the courage of men fails, when we forsake our friends and break all bonds of fellowship, but it is not this day". It's not just a question of the speech made when the good guys face insurmountable odds, although that's often stirring in itself. It's also not just a question of knowing that the forthcoming fight brings an admission of frailty or the only way out. If it were that and that alone, then any corny, low rent film or play would count as great and the speeches within, powerful. But that's not how it is. There has to be a magic something, a sprinkling of something that creates power and inspiration: the way the lines are delivered, how the music blends or soars, how the camera works, how the actor gestures, the story that's gone before, whether we actually care about the individuals and how the language powers the film or play forward. A film can't always deliver the same as a play and vice versa. The medium in each case is very different and people go to one or the other with very different aspirations and expectations.

In both films and plays there are disagreements about what denotes "best". What we're looking for in this book are films and plays in which there are brilliant, inspirational speeches. Of course, this is highly subjective and for every inclusion in this one hundred there are many more films and plays which contain inspirational moments. But we have to begin somewhere. Brilliance and inspiration are not always subjective, of course, and there are some films and plays which most people would regard as good or great and a number of speeches in them as inspirational.

In isolation a speech can't really thrive. The characters have to be believable, the story has to hold strong and the audience has to understand the context fully and why the speech is made. We need to understand and empathise with the characters and care about the heroes. The moment of any speech has to be a hinge upon which the revelation of the tale rests. In this book, you'll see some speeches that stand alone and others that require knowledge of the whole play or film. That's why in each case there's a brief explanation of the story. Because there are only a hundred ideas for your delectation here I've had to concentrate on predominantly English-speaking material, for which I wholeheartedly apologise. Also, most of the examples are from plays and films that are reasonably well known and, I think, have stood (or will stand) the test of time. I must also clarify that not all the chosen items are actually speeches, but sometimes simply a few lines that speak volumes. I make no apology for that since a speech doesn't need length to motivate or captivate.

How do I know what'll inspire you? I don't. But I know what inspires me and many people I know and I hope you'll agree. "Why," you may ask in a minute, "is the author taking me on a tour of the decades from the 1930s to the present day?" The answer is that it's very hard to address a hundred of anything with historical relevance without reference to the period and what was happening at the time. Context is usually important.

One thing for which I should apologise, but won't, is that I do rather give plots and endings away. I ummed and ahhed about this, but came to the conclusion that my "moments" of inspiration wouldn't always make a lot of sense otherwise. I know that I have omitted many brilliant plays and fantastic movies, and erred on the side of films over plays, but that's just the way it's panned out. I wanted to spend time on some of my favourite moments that inspired *me,* and then, having shared them with my children, I wanted to share them with you. I can only hope that my choice is, in part at least, the same as yours.

Chapter One

THE 1930s

Challenging MGM bosses in the 1930s, actress Myrna Loy said: "Why does every black person in the movies have to play a servant? How about a black person walking up the steps of a court house carrying a briefcase?"

"You think I'm licked. You all think I'm licked. Well, I'm *not* licked, and I'm gonna stay right here and fight for this lost cause even if this room gets filled with lies like these … Somebody'll listen to me …" Jefferson Smith (James Stewart) from *Mr. Smith Goes to Washington* (1939)

The Thirties saw the Great Depression in America that spread around the world. It was also the time when authoritarian regimes kept rising, the most well known being Germany's Third Reich and then Mussolini's Italy. The result of these events led to World War II by the end of the decade. The period also saw other major conflicts across the world, including the Spanish Civil War (1936–39), the Chinese Civil War (first one from 1927–37 and the second from 1946–49) and the Sino-Japanese War (1937–45). Countries such as Germany, Italy and Japan exited the The League of Nations, leading to its collapse.

Notable literature included: William Faulkner's *As I lay Dying* (1930); Aldous Huxley's *Brave New World* (1932); F. Scott Fitzgerald's *Tender is the Night* (1934); J.R.R. Tokein's *The Hobbit* (1937) and John Steinbeck's *Of Mice and Men* (1937) and *Grapes of Wrath* (1939).

In the world of films, the decade became known as Hollywood's

Golden Age. Ubi Iwerks produced the first colour and sound cartoon in 1930; the same year, Warner Brothers released *Song of the Flame* directed by Alan Crosland. It was the very first all-talking, all-colour, wide-screen film. The talkies had been introduced in 1927 and full-colour films in 1930. Important characters were introduced in comics. Superman first appeared in 1938, and Batman in 1939. Judy Garland appeared as Dorothy in the movie *The Wizard of Oz* (1939) and Clark Gable played Rhett Butler in *Gone with the Wind* (1939). Walt Disney offered the very first feature-length animated film, *Snow White and the Seven Dwarfs* in 1937.

It was also a time of some great new plays, including *Rise and Fall of the City of Mahogany* and *The Decision* by Bertolt Brecht, *Elisabeth of England* by Ferdinand Bruckner and Noel Coward's *Private Lives,* all in 1930. The following year, Cherokee playwright Lynn Riggs saw her play *Green Grow the Lilacs* premier in the US. It would later be adapted by Rodgers and Hammerstein as the evergreen *Oklahoma!* A number of important plays came to fruition in 1933, including Federico Garcia Lorca's *Blood Wedding,* and Yeats delivered a powerful collection, *The Winding Stair and Other Poems.*

Penguin Books published the first paperback in 1935. That same year several good plays were launched, including T.S. Eliot's *Murder in the Cathedral,* Lawrence Riley's (*Personal Appearance*) and Emlyn Williams' *Night Must Fall.* In 1938 we saw exciting theatre such as Jean Anouilh's *Thieves' Carnival,* and Patrick Hamilton's now famous *Gas Light.* 1939 saw another interesting clutch of plays the likes of *The Philadelphia Story* by Philip Barry, *Arsenic and Old Lace* by Joseph Kesseling and Bertolt Brecht's brilliant *Mother Courage and Her Children.*

The 1930s were lacklustre years for British musical theatre, with the exception of the (arguable) talent that was Noel Coward: *Private Lives* (1930), *Cavalcade (*1931) and *Design For Living (1933).* The decade also saw the Broadway revue reach unprecedented heights of colour, creativity, depth of direction and popularity. Cole Porter had more hit Broadway musicals in the 1930s than any other songwriter. George and Ira Gershwin turned out six shows in the 1930s, including *Strike Up the Band* (1930), a political satire that had the United States and Switzerland go to war over high chocolate tariffs (yes – honestly). *Girl Crazy* (1930) told of a rich New York playboy falling in love with an Arizona cowgirl (absolutely true). The first of Berkeley's choreographed-directed musicals for Warner Brothers was Lloyd Bacon's wonderful *42nd Street* (1933).

New stars who emerged this decade included Jean Harlow, Greta Garbo and Bette Davis. Spencer Tracy won consecutive Best Actor Oscars in the late 1930s for *Captains Courageous* (1937) and *Boys Town* (1938). Exotic German actress Marlene Dietrich's stardom was launched by *The Blue Angel* (Germany, 1929, directed by von Sterberg) where she portrayed the leggy Lola Lola, a cabaret striptease dancer, and by her throaty rendition of *Falling in Love Again.* Two Victor Fleming directed films, *The Wizard of Oz* (1939) and *Gone with the Wind* (1939), were expensively produced in the new Technicolor.

From the mid-'30s onwards there was growing output from directors from outside the US who became famous, such as Jean Renoir, Jean-Luc Godard, Francois Truffaut, David Lean, Roberto Rossellini, Federico Fellini, Vittorio DeSica, Ingmar Bergman, Sergei Eisenstein and Akira Kurosawa. Alfred Hitchcock (from the UK), who had already directed over a dozen films before 1935, brought out spy-chase thrillers: *The Man Who Knew Too Much* (1934), *The 39 Steps* (1935) and *The Lady Vanishes* (1938).

And lastly, the Motion Picture Production Code was developed in 1930, enforced as the Production Code Administration in 1934 (known as The Code or the Hays Code after the originator Will H. Hays). This important legislation (not least because, as a censorial piece of ruling, it diminished creativity) had a very strong hold on what was allowed and what not in films. It set guidelines regarding sex, violence, religion and crime. It purported to uphold America's morals. And on that dampish note, what of inspiration? Let's see.

FROM THE FILM

1 ALL QUIET ON THE WESTERN FRONT

DIRECTED BY LEWIS MILESTONE (1930)

This is an extraordinary (possibly the first) anti-war film with sound and is based on the 1929 novel of the same name by Erich Maria Remarque. The film won Academy Awards for Best Picture and Best Director.

THE STORY

The prologue to the film is more or less taken from the beginning of the novel:

"This story is neither an accusation nor a confession, and least of all an adventure, for death is not an adventure to those who stand face to face with it. It will try simply to tell of a generation of men who, even though they may have escaped its shells, were destroyed by the war …"

The film builds from the pre-war education of German schoolboys and then the enlistment of recruits into the army, focusing on a group of friends. They are caught up in the inspirational zeal with which Germany took to arms. We see the soldiers' shock as they arrive at the Western Front and their inspiration and patriotism turn to deep horror and terror as they experience trench warfare.

One particularly moving and poignant moment is when the doomed protagonist Lew Ayres (Paul Baumer) stretches from his trench to catch a butterfly.

THE SPEECH

There are two particularly interesting inspirational speeches, each from an opposite viewpoint. Professor Kantorek (Arnold Lucy) tells his class of young German hopefuls about the glory of German patriotism. It's meant to urge these boys to seemingly important valour and the glory of dying for the Fatherland:

"... You are the life of the Fatherland, you boys – you are the iron men of Germany … It is not for me to suggest that any of you should stand up and offer to defend his country. But I wonder if such a thing is going through your heads? I know that in one of the schools, the boys have risen up in the classroom and enlisted in a mass … Perhaps, some will say that you should not be allowed to go yet, that you are too young, that you have homes, mothers, fathers, that you should not be torn away. Are your fathers so forgetful of their Fatherland that they would let it perish rather than you? … And after all, is a little experience such a bad thing for a boy? Is the honor of wearing a uniform something from which we should run? … Here is a glorious beginning for your lives!”

Then there is an equally inspirational speech given by Paul Baumer when he returns from war to talk to the professor's class of more young hopefuls. The inspiration here is about despair, but through the despair comes a message that might translate into the hope that not everyone will always make the same mistakes (particularly poignant in hindsight):

“I can't tell you anything you don't know. We live in the trenches out there. We fight. We try not to be killed. Sometimes we are. That's all … I heard you in here reciting that same old stuff, making more iron men, more young heroes. You still think it's beautiful and sweet to die for your country, don't you? … There are millions out there dying for their country, and what good is it? ... I shouldn't have come on leave … Three years we've had of it … And we sleep and eat with death …I shouldn't have come on leave. I'll go back tomorrow. I've got four days more, but I can't stand it here. I'll go back tomorrow.”

FROM THE FILM

2 A FREE SOUL

DIRECTED BY CLARENCE BROWN (1931)

Based on a play and novel of the same name, the former by Willard Mack and the latter by Adela Rogers St. Johns, this is a pre-Code film which meant that the producers decided that anything went, within reason. The film showed a meeting of the new, sexually aware American woman and the newer, tougher American man and provided a brilliant vehicle for Norma Shearer, Clark Gable, Leslie Howard and Lionel Barrymore, who won an Academy Award for Best Actor.

THE STORY

Stephen Ashe (Lionel Barrymore) is a wealthy, successful and alcoholic defence lawyer. As he successfully defends local mobster Ace Wilfong (Clark Gable) in a murder case, his wild daughter Jan (Norma Shearer) breaks her engagement to polo player Dwight Winthrop (Leslie Howard) and starts an affair with Wilfong. However Jan discovers that the liaison is not easily broken off when she's had enough. Winthrop earns her gratitude (and affection) by killing Wilfong – removing a thug and preserving Jan's honour.

THE SPEECH

Stephen Ashe is defending Dwight Winthrop on the charge of the murder of Ace Wilfong, arguing for temporary insanity (because of Ace's lethal threats), although Dwight claims non-payment of a gambling debt as the reason for the murder. Ashe's client is acquitted, but Ashe collapses of a heart attack as he completes his eloquent defence. It's particularly moving because Ashe delivers the speech as if he had no relationship with any of the characters. He clutches at our own heartstrings, not in a slushy or patronising way, but on several fronts. Firstly, we know that he's an alcoholic and is desperately fighting his own demons. Secondly, he's speaking about his wilful daughter whom he adores and about whose future he is terrified. Finally, he has become totally aware that perhaps many of the mistakes made by his daughter are down to him:

"... I'm going to ask you to listen with your hearts. Dwight Winthrop knew that from the cradle on, through all her years, Jan Ashe listened to one man, only one, her father ... You who have sons should pray that they might have the nobility and kindness of this young man. And you who have daughters must believe with him that she was not to blame. It was through her father that she met this gambler, this beast. Her father endorsed this unholy friendship, and when this man threatened the rest of her life, this father wasn't there to protect his daughter. All this Dwight Winthrop knew … The poor boy went insane. And he's not guilty of cold, deliberate murder. There's only one breast that you can surely pin the responsibility of this crime on. Only one! Stephen Ashe is guilty and nobody else. Stephen Ashe. Your honour. I …"

It's a raw speech, yes – a brilliant speech, particularly since we only realise after a while that he's talking about himself.

FROM THE FILM

3 42ND STREET

DIRECTED BY LLOYD BACON (1933)

This film, adapted from the novel of the same name by Bradford Ropes, captured the hearts and imagination of many during the post-Depression era. Here was a Cinderella-like tale of an inexperienced chorus girl who made it by luck into the cast of a big stage show, stepped into the leading role under fortuitous circumstances, and then won acclaim for that role. Some fifty years after the movie was made, *42nd Street* became a hit Broadway stage musical of the same name and is still drawing crowded houses and rave reviews.

THE STORY

Julian Marsh (Warner Baxter) is a successful Broadway director suffering from poor health. He produces a new show called *Pretty Lady*, financed by a rich old man, Billy Lawlor (Dick Powell), who's in love with the star of the show, Dorothy Brock (Bebe Daniels). The night before the show's opening, Dorothy Brock twists her ankle and one of the chorus girls, Peggy Sawyer (Ruby Keeler), gets the opportunity to take over her part.

THE SPEECH

Marsh instructs novice Sawyer to go out and become a star. What he says is one of the most famous exhortations in film (or theatre) history:

> “Now Sawyer, you listen to me and you listen hard. Two hundred people, two hundred jobs, two hundred thousand dollars, five weeks of grind and blood and sweat depend upon you … You've got to go on and you have to give and give and give. They've got to like you, they've got to … You can't fall down. You can't, because your future's in it, my future and everything all of us have is staked on you … But you keep your feet on the ground and your head on those shoulders of yours and go out – and Sawyer, you're going out a youngster, but you've got to come back a star.”

Naturally, the show is a success and in the final scene Marsh goes out of the theatre and sits exhausted on a step relieved and delighted. We are with him and feel for him. Without his inspiring speech to the young Peggy, the end of the film wouldn't be nearly so powerful.

FROM THE FILM

4 RUGGLES OF RED GAP

DIRECTED BY LEO MCCAREY (1935)

Patriotic love of an adopted country is a great way of underlining how great the adopted country is. Previously filmed in 1918 and 1923, Harry Leon Wilson's novel of the same name (1915) achieved movie classic status in the 1935 remake and was filmed for a fourth time in 1950 as the Bob Hope-Lucille Ball musical, *Fancy Pants*.

THE STORY

During a poker game in Paris in 1908, Lord Burnstead (Roland Young) uses his butler, Marmaduke Ruggles (Charles Laughton) as a bet and loses the game and his butler. Egbert (Charles Ruggles) and Effie Floud (Mary

Boland) bring Marmaduke Ruggles back to Red Gap, Washington. Effie wants to take advantage of Ruggles' posh, upper class background to influence Egbert's hick and somewhat common lifestyle. Egbert, who's more interested in partying, takes Ruggles to a local bar and introduces him as a colonel. The local newspaper makes out that a Colonel Ruggles is staying with close friends, the Flouds. He becomes a local celebrity and opens a restaurant. His transition from servant to an independent man of means will depend on its success. One of his first customers is his previous boss, Lord Burnstead. A simple, heartwarming, inspirational story and enormous fun.

THE SPEECH

The longer he spends in America, the more Ruggles likes the American concept of democracy and self-determination, where somebody can be anything. He tells people at the Silver Dollar Saloon that he was inspired by "what Lincoln said at Gettysburg" and then recites The Gettysburg Address. He begins softly and then reaches a higher volume and crescendo as more and more bar patrons listen in astonishment and some wonder. This is a powerful, moving and inspirational scene.

> "Four score and seven years ago our fathers brought forth on this continent, a new nation, conceived in Liberty and dedicated to the proposition that all men are created equal …"

Read it if you don't know it. It's a brilliant piece of rhetoric in any context. In the context of the film, it's stupendous.

From the film

5 MR. DEEDS GOES TO TOWN

directed by Frank Capra (1936)

Capra won his second Academy Award (out of three) as Best Director with this film. A short-lived ABC television series of the same name ran from 1969 to 1970, starring Monte Markham as Longfellow Deeds. It was also remade as *Mr. Deeds* in 2002, starring Adam Sandler and Winona Ryder. The pleasure of the 1936 film, adapted by Robert Riskin from Clarence Buddington Kelland's short story, *Opera Hat,* is watching the country bumpkin outwit city slickers and seeing some great actors acting superbly well.

THE STORY

A wealthy patron of the arts dies in a car crash, leaving a twenty-million-dollar fortune to Longfellow Deeds (Gary Cooper), who is already a successful businessman and doesn't really need the money. Deeds is persuaded to move to New York where he meets tough reporter Babe Bennett (Jean Arthur) who follows him everywhere, writing stories about Deeds' no nonsense behaviour that make the headlines, but aren't always pleasant to or for Deeds. But then she falls in love with him. Meanwhile Deeds has set up a foundation to help America's needy people, providing they help themselves. His lawyer John Cedar (Douglas Dumbrille) thinks that Deeds is nuts and tries to have him declared insane. At the court hearing, the judge recommends that Deeds should be committed for his own safety. Disillusioned, Deeds doesn't fight back. Babe begs him to and in court professes her love for and to him and then testifies on his behalf. Listening to the case is a crowd of farmers who support Deeds because of what he's trying to do for people in tough times. With this kind of support, Deeds realises that he needs to stand up for himself and so defends his philanthropic motives. What we get next is a superb and inspirational argument which makes the soul soar and the eyes damp.

THE SPEECH

Deeds argues that those who have money should help those who don't. And this is the crunch rhetoric that is so important as a brilliant speech in its own right:

"... From what I can see ... there will always be leaders and always be followers. It's like the road out in front of my house. It's on a steep hill. Every day I watch the cars climbing up. Some go lickety-split up that hill on high, some have to shift into second and some sputter and shake and slip back to the bottom again. Same cars, same gasoline, yet some make it and some don't. And I say the fellas who can make the hill on high should stop once in a while and help those who can't. That's all I'm trying to do with this money. Help the fellas who can't make the hill on high ... ”

FROM THE FILM

6 THE LIFE OF ÉMILE ZOLA

DIRECTED BY WILLIAM DIETERLE (1937)

This film was a commercial success and also won an Academy Award for Best Picture. While it is certainly not a completely reliable historical account, it paints a good picture of the times, focuses well on a heroic deed, and offers some stirring speeches.

It's worth remembering that events depicted in the film, most of which took place between 1894 and 1902, were still within living memory in 1937. The real Dreyfus died in 1935, outliving everyone else involved in the case.

THE STORY

French writer Zola (Paul Muni) is starving in a Parisian garret along with his painter friend, Paul Cézanne (Vladimir Sokoloff). Zola writes what he sees as social and political truths, but his work is seen as provocative and censored. He achieves fame and fortune with a book about a prostitute. The film is devoted to Zola's attempts to clear the reputation of army captain Alfred Dreyfus (Joseph Schildkraut), who has been framed on a charge of treason by the French army, and condemned to Devil's Island. Publishing his famous manifesto, "J'accuse", Zola is condemned publicly for siding with a so-called traitor. He is prosecuted and, although he delivers a brilliant self-defence, is found guilty. He flees to England and continues to rail against the corrupt military establishment of France, eventually forcing a retrial of Dreyfus and subsequent pardon.

THE SPEECH

There are two parts of this film that deserve a mention here. Zola brings charges of army corruption, in an open letter to the president of France, about the Dreyfus affair:

> “I shall tell the truth ... Dreyfus knows several languages – crime. He works hard – crime. No compromising papers are found in his apartment – crime. He goes occasionally to the country of his origin – crime. He endeavors to learn everything – crime. He's not easily worried – crime. He is easily worried – also a crime ... For over a year, the Minister of War and the General Staff have known that Dreyfus is innocent, but they've kept this knowledge to themselves. And those men sleep and they have wives and children they love.”

This is followed by a series of famous “I Accuse” statements and his final plea:

> “... Let there be a trial in the full light of day! I am waiting.”

The inspiration is palpable – if, for nothing else, that a man will show humanity to another man, caring not about the risk to himself. Secondly, *The Life of Émile Zola* deserves classic status due to Paul Muni's simply superb performance as Zola. Here he defends Captain Dreyfus for alleged espionage:

> “... Not only is an innocent man crying out for justice, but more – much more – a great nation is in desperate danger of forfeiting her honour. Do not take upon yourselves a fault, the burden of which you will forever bear in history ... And now, today, you're asked to condemn me because I rebelled on seeing our country embarked on this terrible course. At this solemn moment in the presence of this tribunal, which is the representative of human justice ... before France, before the whole world, I swear that Dreyfus is innocent.”

Well, to be very naughty, we'll slip in another speech here although we won't give it a separate number. It's the eulogy on Zola given by his friend, Paul Cézanne. It's vibrant, stirring and, once again, an example of great oratory. It fits the epithet "inspirational" and finishes thus:

"Let us not pity him because he suffered and endured. Let us envy him. Let us envy him because his great heart won him the proudest of destinies: he was a moment of the conscience of man."

FROM THE FILM

7 GONE WITH THE WIND

DIRECTED BY VICTOR FLEMING (1939)

Although not everyone's cup of tea, this film is a landmark epic drama following great tranches of American history and is also reasonably faithful to the book by Margaret Mitchell (1936). Certainly the production values are superb, the acting works and it made superstars of many of its players long before the word was invented. The film also won ten Academy Awards.

THE STORY

The film is set during the American Civil War (1861–65) and is essentially about a selfish and spoilt woman, Scarlett O'Hara (Vivien Leigh), whose father (Thomas Mitchell) owns a plantation (called Tara) in Georgia. Scarlett fancies Ashley Wilkes (Lesley Howard), but he's to be married to his cousin, Melanie Hamilton (Olivia de Havilland). At the party announcing Ashley's engagement to Melanie, Scarlett meets Rhett Butler (Clark Gable), who's something of a worldly-wise rogue.

The Civil War begins and Scarlett agrees to marry Charles Hamilton (Rand Brooks), who soon dies of pneumonia and measles. She later marries Frank Kennedy (Carroll Nye) in order to pay taxes on Tara, which she inherited from her father. When Frank dies in a fight with troops, Scarlett marries Rhett, who is aware of her passion for Ashley, but hopes that one day she will come to love him instead. Scarlett eventually comes to realise that she does love Rhett, but only when it's apparently too late. Rhett, not giving the proverbial damn, gives up waiting for her love and leaves. She returns to Tara to think of a way to get him back.

THE SPEECH

After Atlanta is attacked by Union troops and she has delivered Melanie's baby with the help of a servant, Prissy (Butterfly McQueen), Scarlett asks Rhett to take her home to Tara with Melanie, Prissy and the baby. When they get there, Tara has been deserted by all except her father (who's losing his mind), her sisters and a couple of servants. The place has been stripped of many valuables by the Union troops and the fields are overgrown. In silhouette against a beautiful sunset, she says:

> “As God is my witness, as God is my witness, they're not going to lick me! I'm going to live through this, and when it's all over, I'll never be hungry again – no, nor any of my folks! If I have to lie, steal, cheat or kill, as God is my witness, I'll never be hungry again.”

It's a rousing speech and certainly inspirational, and, much as we may not like Scarlett, it works. Pure whimsy forces the inclusion of another major piece of rhetoric – the famous closing monologue after Rhett Butler's dismissive departure where Scarlett says:

> “I can't let him go. I can't. There must be some way to bring him back. Oh I can't think about this now! … I'll think about it tomorrow. But I must think about it … What is there to do? What is there that matters? ... Tara! ... Home. I'll go home and I'll think of some way to get him back! After all, tomorrow is another day!”

FROM THE FILM

8 MR. SMITH GOES TO WASHINGTON

DIRECTED BY FRANK CAPRA (1939)

Despite pressure from politicians (including Joseph Kennedy) to have this film withdrawn and the fact that American newspapers and journalists resented how they were portrayed, this film became one of Capra's most successful works – perhaps even the most successful – and was much liked outside the US because it shows how a democracy could openly criticise democracy.

The film shows that even with the downturn and financial crisis, America had ideals for which it would fight. That struck a chord and the appeal of the film has kept growing. Writer Lewis R. Foster won an Academy Award – for Best Writing, Original Story.

THE STORY

The patriotic young and inexperienced Senator Jefferson Smith (James Stewart) wants legislation to buy some land in his home state for a national boys' camp, to be paid back by youngsters across America. The legislation is passed and money pours in for the scheme. However, the proposed campsite is already part of a dam building scheme included in a Public Works bill framed by the immoral and greedy industrial magnate Jim Taylor (Edward Arnold) and Senator Paine (Claude Rains). Taylor attempts first to buy Smith off, then plans to break him. Smith is framed and will be seen as dishonest unless he proves his innocence. He defends himself and, in the climactic scene, challenges both the political machine and the Senate itself by filibustering (making a prolonged speech that obstructs legislative progress, while not technically contravening the required procedures) in the Senate for twenty-three hours, finally appealing to the now conscious-stricken Paine. Faith and vindication of Smith's idealism win out and we all cheer.

THE SPEECH

In the filibuster speech, Stewart is in turn defensive, uncertain, defiant, wounded and inspired. It's his beliefs that we like.

Towards the film's end and in one of the most powerful scenes ever, Smith staggers forward in disbelief to look at the myriad of telegrams that his enemies have forged. He looks desperate and alone – then turns towards Senator Paine to deliver an impassioned speech about the betrayal of ideals:

"I guess this is just another lost cause, Mr. Paine. All you people don't know about the lost causes. Mr. Paine does. He said once they were the only causes worth fighting for. And he fought for them once, for the only reason that any man ever fights for them. Because of just one plain simple rule: 'Love thy neighbour.' And in this world today, full of hatred, a man who knows that one rule has a great trust. You know that rule, Mr. Paine. And I loved you for it, just as my father did. And you know that you fight for the lost causes harder than for any others. Yes, you even die for them. Like a man we both knew, Mr. Paine."

And, of course, we get closure. The wicked Paine confesses and Smith is vindicated as a hero.

AN OVERVIEW OF CHAPTER ONE

There are moving speeches in the theatre and film and there are those that just make us reflect. We consider our own lives or we compare them with others'. We wonder at the sorry state of viewed lives or the huge happiness we see expressed. We like to learn what makes some people able to come through catastrophes, while others, apparently just as able and brave, struggle. In *Gone With the Wind*, Scarlett and Rhett are survivors because they adapt to the changes brought about by the war and America's Reconstruction.

In general, many great speeches from the world of film or theatre show that we shouldn't waste time (or our lives) chasing after a dream that doesn't really exist, or an illusion that doesn't really matter. We should spend time on those things that *do* matter or which have moral value. *Mr. Deeds Goes to*

Town and *Mr Smith Goes to Washington* both make us feel good because they reflect morals and hopes in which we all believe, even the most cynical of us.

Many of us are cynical about films of war. The film *All Quiet on the Western Front* is a classic Hollywood adaptation of Erich Remarque's remarkable novel. It takes a hard look at the tragedy of war with World War I as its backdrop. World War I films are perhaps more abstract than those relating to more recent conflicts. The lines of good and bad are much less clearly drawn. In fact, a lot of the isolationism seen during the Thirties stemmed from the impression that the Great War was fought over little and concluded nothing. In *42nd Street*, the Busby Berkeley choreography is fabulous – no one ever did it like this. There's a satisfying sexiness and beauty in the dance routines and that alone makes us smile. A lot got by the censors in this film to the delight of the audiences, although things were tightened up the following year as the Hayes Office started to crack down.

Mr. Deeds Goes to Town has a pace that never lets the viewer down. In comparison with what often passes today as film comedy, this is a masterpiece. We like the story because we can identify with Mr. Deeds and this pulls us through all the way to the predictable, yet delightful and satisfying conclusion.

But, of course, in mirroring life, some stories don't have a happy ending and we need those too to allow us to think, ponder, compare and stop us in our tracks.

Emile Zola stopped Paris and a country in its tracks. He felt that the rights of one man were sufficiently important to inconvenience and embarrass an entire nation. Seeing goodness and selflessness in others is humbling and perhaps that humility is shared. In *The Life of Émile Zola*, we are absorbed, we smile and are saddened (although not in equal measure); feelings that are cathartic. And inspirational.

Chapter Two

THE 1940s

Al Joad: "Ain't you gonna look back, Ma? Give the ol' place a last look?"
Ma Joad: "We're going to California, ain't we? All right then, let's go to California."
Al Joad: "That don't sound like you, Ma. You never was like that before."
Ma Joad: "I never had my house pushed over before. Never had my family stuck out on the road. Never had to lose everything I had in life."
Ma Joad (Jane Darwell) and Al Joad (O.Z. Whitehead) frrom the film *The Grapes of Wrath* (1940)

The end of World War II in 1945 marked the beginning of the East-West conflict and the Cold War. One of the gains from the war was the United Nations, established to help negotiate and manage future world conflicts, even though it was shown to have blunt teeth. India gained independence from the UK in 1947 and Pakistan in the same year. In 1948, after achieving independence for India, Mahatma Gandhi was assassinated. 1948 also saw the Arab-Israeli war develop almost immediately as the new state of Israel came into being. In 1949, NATO was formed by the major western powers for collective security. *For Whom the Bell Tolls* was published by Ernest Hemingway in 1940, *The Little Prince* by Antoine de Saint-Expury in 1943, *No Exit* by Jean-Paul Sartre in 1944, *The Diary of Anne Frank* in 1947, and both Arthur Miller's play *Death of a Salesman* and George Orwell's *Nineteen Eighty Four* in 1949.

The decade saw the development of the Colossus computer, used by

British code breakers to read encrypted German messages during World War II. The first test (called Trinity) of an atomic device was made as part of Robert Oppenheimer's Manhattan Project, the result of which was the bomb which ended Japan's war. Radar was invented during the 1940s, as was the jet aircraft and the Jeep. Commercial television also began.

Top films of the 1940s included *The Grapes of Wrath* (1940), *Citizen Kane* (1941), *Casablanca (*1942), *Shadow of a Doubt* (1943), *Double Indemnity (*1944), *It's a Wonderful Life* (1946), *The Red Shoes* (1948) and *The Third Man* (1949). Films took on more realistic themes than they had in escapist 30s. In 1944 Laurence Olivier directed and starred in a film version of *Henry V*, which was a worldwide success and won Olivier an Honorary Academy Award for outstanding achievement. Britain's biggest sex-symbol in the late 1940s was Diana Dors, whose first notable screen performance was in David Lean's *Oliver Twist* (1948) with Alec Guinness as Fagin.

The 1940s also offered patriotic entertainment such as William Wyler's inspirational and hugely powerful war-time film, *Mrs. Miniver* (1942). Inspiration was a major theme in many films. WW II drama, *In Which We Serve* (1942), co-directed by David Lean and Noël Coward, paid tribute to the Royal Navy. *Since You Went Away* (1944) directed by John Cromwell was the American version of *Mrs. Miniver.*

Most people either love or loathe Charlie Chaplin. He directed and starred in his first talking picture, *The Great Dictator* (1940), which succeeded perhaps more on content than on acting skills. Marlene Dietrich (another acquired taste) made a number of morale-boosting films and the Spanish Civil War served as the backdrop for the film version of Hemmingway's *For Whom the Bell Tolls (*1943), directed by Sam Wood and starring Gary Cooper and Ingrid Bergman.

Some of the most popular box-office stars of the decade include Clark Gable, Judy Garland, Bette Davis, Bing Crosby, Humphrey Bogart, Cary Grant and Ingrid Bergman. Twelve-year-old child actress Elizabeth Taylor became a star after making *Lassie Come Home* (1943) and *National Velvet* (1944). Tyrone Power gave an outstanding performance as heroic Don Diego Vega, son of a 19th century aristocrat, better known as Zorro, in *The Mark of Zorro* (1940) directed by Rouben Mamoulian. The same year, Errol Flynn buckled his swash as privateer Captain Geoffrey Thorpe, better known as *The Sea Hawk* in the action film by director Michael Curtiz. Humphrey Bogart didn't become a major Hollywood star until 1941, after he had played a few gangsters and appeared in John Huston's *The Maltese Falcon* (1941).

Citizen Kane (1941) was co-written, directed by and starred Orson Welles. It's regarded by some as the best film ever made – not a view shared by everyone. Welles also acted as the enigmatic Harry Lime and provided the famous cuckoo clock speech in director Carol Reed's British classic, *The Third Man* (1949).

The much loved Paramount Studios' Road films (seven in all stretching until 1962), starred Bob Hope and Bing Crosby as two hapless musicians with their heroine, Dorothy Lamour. American comedy became a good, soothing tonic for post-war blues, not only in the States, but around the world. Dry humour was one of the hallmarks of the Katharine Hepburn and Spencer Tracy pairing. And the evergreen Christmas favourite, *Miracle on 34th Street* (1947, directed by George Seaton and then made again in 1994, that version directed by Les Mayfield) suited the mood. Frank Capra idealised the common man in his first independent production called *Meet John Doe* (1941) starring Gary Cooper, but the film for which he is perhaps best known is the perennial Christmas film, *It's a Wonderful Life* (1946), which is indeed inspirational, wonderful and life affirming. The '40s also saw the introduction of many cartoon figures we still find enchanting today, including: Bugs Bunny, Tom and Jerry and Woody Woodpecker. The golden decade of Disney animation was heralded by *Pinocchio* (1940). Other Disney feature-length animations included *Dumbo* (1941) and *Bambi* (1942).

Macarthyism raised its ugly head and many in Hollywood, including Orson Welles, Gregory Peck, Katharine Hepburn, Gene Kelly, Frank Sinatra, Arthur Miller and Charlie Chaplin were either falsely accused of being Communist sympathisers or alleged to be part of a Communist network for refusing to answer questions. Times were tough, but a real exponent of truly tough times was the film, *Grapes of Wrath*.

FROM THE FILM

9 THE GRAPES OF WRATH

DIRECTED BY JOHN FORD (1940)

This film won two Academy Awards, including one for John Ford's direction. The title of the superb black and white epic drama, adapted from John Steinbeck's 1939 Pulitzer Prize-winning novel of the same name, was taken from *Battle Hymn of the Republic*, by Julia Ward Howe:

"Mine eyes have seen the glory of the coming of the Lord,
He is trampling out the vintage where the grapes of wrath are stored,
He has loosed the fateful lightning of His terrible swift sword,
His truth is marching on".

THE STORY

This direct and honest film focused on the deep impact of the Great Depression, particularly on one family, the Joads, whose plight depicted thousands of farmers' struggles during the period. Many small-holders in Oklahoma, Colorado, Texas and Kansas were closed down by the banks or bought up by large farm businesses. Families were forced to search westward for some sort of American Dream.

After serving four years in prison for killing a man, hotheaded Tom Joad (Henry Fonda), on his way back to his family farm in Oklahoma, meets Casy (John Carradine), a former preacher who has lost his faith. They find the home farm deserted and discover that Tom's family has been evicted. Tom is reunited with his family at his uncle's farm, only to discover the family must also leave that farm the next day. The extended family of eight (plus Casy) packs its belongings onto an old truck and heads for California along Route 66 to look for work.

En route, Grandpa (Charley Grapewin) dies of a stroke. Money is tight; food is scarce. Grandma (Zeffie Tilbury) also dies just before the family reaches the Californian border. At a migrant camp a man and sheriff promise work, but won't say what the pay might be. Someone declares this to be a dishonest ruse and the sheriff tries to arrest the man. The man runs away and the sheriff shoots at him, but kills a bystander instead. Tom knocks out the sheriff and flees. The family also leaves and goes to a farm to pick peaches for next to no money. Casy, who is helping to lead a strike against the farm (which is much like a concentration camp), is killed by some farm thugs, one of whom is then killed by Tom.

Once again, the family moves on, heading north. Life is better at a US government camp, but the sheriff arrives at the camp looking for Tom, who vows to his mother, Ma Joad (Jane Darwell) that he will fight injustice wherever he finds it and heads off into the night. The family hears of work and goes north to find it; an optimistic Ma is hopeful about the future.

THE SPEECH

Towards the end of this extraordinarily powerful and inspirational film, Tom Joad has to escape the law and seek new pastures. He says farewell to Ma Joad and this is the film's core, it's inspiring moment, or certainly one of them:

"... I'll be all around in the dark. I'll be ever'-where – wherever you can look. Wherever there's a fight so hungry people can eat, I'll be there. Wherever there's a cop beatin' up a guy, I'll be there. I'll be in the way guys yell when they're mad – I'll be in the way kids laugh when they're hungry an' they know supper's ready. An' when the people are eatin' the stuff they raise, and livin' in the houses they build – I'll be there, too."

Ma doesn't really understand what her son wants to do although she probably understands why. She believes that suffering is her lot and says to Tom:

"Tom, we – we ain't the kissin' kind, but..."

And they kiss. And then Tom walks away.

From the film
10 MRS. MINIVER
directed by William Wyler (1942)

This was a sensational film in its time and carried great influence on both sides of the Atlantic. More than anything, it made it clear to Americans that Britain needed help. The ending is thought-provoking, inspirational and simply wonderful.

Greer Garson, playing an English rose, gives a superb performance as the devoted and loving wife, Mrs. Miniver. Walter Pidgeon is also great as her husband, Clem. The film offers drama, romance, humour and tragedy, but what marks it out considerably is that it shows humanity and war-time sacrifice without being particularly sugary, sentimental or insipid. The film won six Academy Awards, including Best Actress for Greer Garson, Best Director and Best Picture.

THE STORY

It's the summer of 1939 and we meet Kay Miniver (Greer Garson), her husband Clem (Walter Pidgeon), daughter Judy (Clare Sandars) and toddler son Toby (Christopher Severn). Older son Vin (Richard Ney) soon returns from Oxford University.

We soon see conflicts between various social classes. The Minivers spend beyond their means, perhaps to try and promote their status. Local railway stationmaster James Ballard (Henry Travers) grows a rose that he names the "Mrs. Miniver" after Kay whom he admires. He wants to enter it in a local contest run – and always won – by aristocratic Lady Beldon (Dame May Whitty). Vin rails against the British class system, which brings him into conflict with Lady Beldon's granddaughter Carol (Teresa Wright), although the two are attracted to each other. Her summer departure for Scotland thwarts the romance.

Carol returns from Scotland in September 1939, when the war is beginning to have an impact on the community. The Minivers' maid, Gladys (Brenda Forbes), is distressed when her boyfriend Horace (Rhys Williams) is called up. A year later, Vin becomes a Pilot Officer with the RAF. He and Carol get engaged, but he has to fly almost immediately. Clem Miniver helps retrieve members of the British Expeditionary Force in Dunkirk. The family goes through air raids and other shocks and absurdities of war, including Mrs. Miniver confronting a downed Nazi paratrooper in her kitchen and an annual flower show being staged despite the bombing raids.

The film is a propaganda piece, but nothing detracts from the story and its inspiration. Winston Churchill was apparently moved to comment that its propaganda value was worth a dozen battleships.

THE SPEECH

The vicar (Henry Wilcoxon) makes what is essentially a call to arms in his bombed church before the congregation sings *Onward Christian Soldiers*. In the sermon he posits important questions about duty and loss:

“We in this quiet corner of England have suffered the loss of friends very dear to us, some close to this church. George West, choirboy. James Ballard, stationmaster and bell-ringer and the proud winner only an hour before his death of the Beldon Cup for his beautiful Miniver Rose. And our hearts go out in sympathy to the two families who share the cruel loss of a young girl who was married at this altar only two weeks ago. The homes of many of us have been destroyed and the lives of young and old have been taken. There's scarcely a household that hasn't been struck to the heart. And why? Surely you must have asked yourselves this question? Why in all conscience should these be the ones to suffer? Children, old people, a young girl at the height of her loveliness. Why these? Are these our soldiers? Are these our fighters? Why should they be sacrificed? I shall tell you why. Because this is not only a war of soldiers in uniform. It is a war of the people, of all the people, and it must be fought not only on the battlefield, but in the cities and in the villages, in the factories and on the farms, in the home, and in the heart of every man, woman, and child who loves freedom! Well, we have buried our dead, but we shall not forget them. Instead they will inspire us with an unbreakable determination to free ourselves and those who come after us from the tyranny and terror that threaten to strike us down. This is the people's war! It is our war! We are the fighters! Fight it then! Fight it with all that is in us, and may God defend the right!"

The vicar's speech was translated into many languages and leaflets air-dropped over German-occupied Europe; it was also broadcast over the *Voice of America* and printed in *Time* magazine. It stirred then and it stirs now.

FROM THE FILM

11 CASABLANCA

DIRECTED BY MICHAEL CURTIZ (1942)

The airport farewell scene in this great film must be one of the best known movie moments ever. Set during World War II in the Vichy-controlled Moroccan city of Casablanca, it starred Humphrey Bogart and Ingrid Bergman, whose charismatic and sometimes sizzling performances have been rightly praised. *Casablanca* won three Academy Awards.

THE STORY

To flee the Germans or Germany during the war and seek refuge in the US, many Europeans have to go via Casablanca to obtain exit visas. The best place to be in Casablanca is Rick's Café, run by Rick Blaine (Humphrey Bogart), a sardonic American expatriate who, for some dark reason, can't return to the US.

Two German couriers have been killed and the documents they were carrying stolen. One of Rick's regulars, Ugarte (Peter Lorre), entrusts to him some letters of transit, which he intends to sell but, before he can, is arrested for killing the couriers. Captain Renault (Claude Rains), the Chief of Police, tells Rick that Victor Laszlo (Paul Henreid), the European Resistance leader, is in Casablanca and will do anything to get an exit visa, but Renault has been (confidentially) advised by Gestapo Major Strasser (Conrad Veidt) to keep Laszlo in Casablanca.

Laszlo goes to Rick's to meet Ugarte, as Ugarte was going to sell him the letters. Accompanying him is his beautiful wife, Ilsa Lund (Ingrid Bergman), who knew Rick from Paris. Clearly there's been some history between Ilsa and Rick. Rick refuses to hand over the letters as he doesn't take sides and is only looking after himself anyway. Ilsa begs Rick for help and offers herself in exchange for Laszlo's safe transport. Bitter Rick must decide what is more important – his own happiness or the lives of others. The end sees Rick doing the right thing.

THE SCENE

Rick Blaine makes an airport farewell speech to Ilsa, featuring famous lines:

“Ilsa, I'm no good at being noble, but it doesn't take much to see that the problems of three little people don't amount to a hill of beans in this crazy world. Someday you'll understand that. Now, now. Here's looking at you, kid.”

In a supreme moment of romantic self-sacrifice, he affirms his love for her by urging her to leave Casablanca with her husband and the precious letters of transit that Renault is countersigning:

“Rick: If that plane leaves the ground and you're not with him, you'll regret it.

Ilsa: No.

Rick: Maybe not today and maybe not tomorrow, but soon and for the rest of your life.

Ilsa: What about us?

Rick (romantically): We'll always have Paris. We didn't have – we'd – we'd lost it until you came to Casablanca. We got it back last night.

Ilsa: When I said I would never leave you.

Rick: And you never will. I've got a job to do too. Where I'm going, you can't follow. What I've got to do, you can't be any part of.”

At the film's end, Ilsa and Laszlo walk across the runway to a plane bound for Lisbon, she heading for an unromantic and loveless relationship, he to do his job as a freedom fighter. Lazlo notices her expression and, we assume, understands her feelings for Rick, standing alone on the edge of the runway, his face a mask. Draining and inspirational indeed!

FROM THE MUSICAL AND FILM

12 OKLAHOMA

(BROADWAY MUSICAL IN 1943, FILM IN 1955)

I've chosen a scene more than a speech on this occasion. This was the first musical written by Rodgers and Hammerstein and they received a special Pulitzer Prize for it. Based on Lynn Riggs' 1931 play, *Green Grow the Lilacs*, it is set in Oklahoma, USA, outside the town of Claremore in 1906 and is about cowboy Curly McLain and his romance with farm girl Laurey Williams. The original Broadway production was a box-office hit and ran for over 2,200 performances. In 1955 there was an Academy Award-winning film adaptation.

THE STORY

Curly and Jud, a hired farmhand, vie for the affections of Laurey. They are in an Indian territory of the American West at a time when Oklahoma is to be established as a state. There are class issues between the farmers and cowmen in the still developing, rugged and pioneering environment as the characters struggle to find hope, love and the fulfillment of the American Dream. Curly and Laurey both have feelings for each other, but have difficulty expressing it because of their stubbornness. Just to spite Curly, Laurey accepts an invitation to the local dance from Jud. Eventually, Curly and Jud duel it out. Meanwhile, Will Parker, a simple chap, is desperately in love with Ado Annie Carnes, an equally simple but very flirtatious young lady. Will has returned early from a trip to Kansas City to discover that Ado Annie just can't seem to say no to other men.

THE SCENE

In the second half of the second act, Jud (the bad guy) confronts Laurey (the good gal) about his feelings for her. When she admits that she doesn't return them, he threatens her. She then fires him as her farm hand. Laurey bursts into tears and calls for Curly (the good guy), who is delighted that she has turned to him for help and reassurance. He plucks up his courage and proposes to her; she readily accepts. Cue for a song: the reprise of "People Will Say We're In Love". That could have been that but, of course, it isn't …

This is the point at which the story becomes (more) motivational and, while fun, is truly inspirational as indeed many musicals can be. This is also the point, as in many stories, when good prevails and when we, the audience, just know everything's going to be alright. It's a valuable moment.

Three weeks later, a drunken Jud reappears after Curly and Laurey's wedding. He attacks Curly with a knife. As Curly avoids a blow, Jud falls on his own knife and dies. Laurey's Aunt Eller insists that the wedding guests hold a makeshift trial for Curly as the married couple is due to go on honeymoon. The judge, Ado Annie's father, declares a not guilty verdict and everyone delightedly sings the title song in celebration of that and the territory's impending statehood.

FROM THE PLAY

13 THE GLASS MENAGERIE

WRITTEN BY TENNESSEE WILLIAMS (1944)

This play is said to mirror Williams' own life with himself as the character, Tom. It's a brilliant play with scenes that will move anyone. Two film versions were later made, one in 1950 directed by Irving Rapper and the second directed by Paul Newman in 1987. Neither is regarded as particularly great – certainly not in comparison with the first production of the play onstage. The play, the language, the structure and the raw emotion within are all superbly put together.

THE STORY

Written from Tom's point of recollection, the play features action in the past played as the present. Amanda, the mother who was abandoned some sixteen years earlier by Tom's father, has struggled to bring up Tom and his sister Laura. Once a Southern belle, she clings with some dignity to how things were. Laura has mental difficulties, a crippled foot, and is terrified of the outside world. She spends much of her time with her glass menagerie of tiny glass animals. Tom works in a warehouse to support his mother and sister, but has ambitions to be a writer. Jim O'Connor, Tom's colleague, knows Laura from school and Amanda, who thinks he'd be perfect for Laura, invites him to dinner, and spends what little money they have on making the place nice and the dinner good.

Laura realises she has loved Jim since high school days. After dinner when they dance, he accidentally breaks a glass unicorn. During the course of the evening he tells her he's already engaged to be married and leaves. When Amanda learns this, she takes her fury out on Tom thinking he knew and planned to make fools of mother and daughter. Tom leaves home soon after that and doesn't return. Although he does escape, as his father did, he is still haunted by the memory of the sister he left behind.

THE SPEECH

This is the play's closing speech. One can only urge you to read it in full. Please do. It inspires a huge surge of hope, it beseeches and begs forgiveness, it extols virtue and love and it's supremely affectionate and caring:

“Tom: I didn't go to the moon … Not long after that I was fired for writing a poem on the lid of a shoebox. I left St. Louis … I travelled around a great deal … I would have stopped, but I was pursued by something. It always came upon me unawares, taking me altogether by surprise … Then all at once my sister touches my shoulder. I turn around and look into her eyes. Oh Laura, Laura, I tried to leave you behind me, but I am more faithful than I intended to be! I reach for a cigarette, I cross the street … anything that can blow your candles out! [Laura bends over the candles] For nowadays the world is lit by lightning! Blow out your candles, Laura – and so goodbye ... [She blows the candles out]"

FROM THE FILM

14 TO HAVE AND HAVE NOT

DIRECTED BY HOWARD HAWKS (1944)

This film is a wartime adventure loosely based on Ernest Hemingway's 1937 novel of the same name. Warner Brothers decided that it needed to follow up their earlier success of *Casablanca,* so a story was chosen with a similar set of ingredients: interesting location (the Caribbean), an unmarried expatriate tough American with a heart of gold deep down, a love interest, resistance fighters, a Gestapo police captain, a café and, of course, a piano player.

This film paired (the then married) Humphrey Bogart and a nineteen year-old Lauren Bacall for the first time.

THE STORY

It is 1940 and France has fallen. Harry (Steve) Morgan (Humphrey Bogart) and his inebriated sidekick, Eddie (Walter Brennan) find that business in the boat rental business in Martinique is poor because of the war. A customer defaults on paying a debt to Harry so he and Eddie are obliged to take whatever comes their way. A hotel owner, Gerard, known as Frenchy (Marcel Dalio) and the leader of the Gaulist Free French, asks Harry to rent him his boat for one night to transport two underground resistance fugitives, Helene (Dolores Moran) and Paul de Bursac (Walter Szurovy) to Martinique. Meanwhile a relationship blossoms between Harry and Marie (Slim) Browning (Lauren Bacall), a drifting American who is staying on the island. During the boat trip with the fugitives, Paul is shot in the shoulder. Harry removes the bullet and Paul asks Harry to help a man escape from Devil's Island, but Harry isn't interested.

The police, who recognise Harry's boat, tell him that they have Eddie in custody and try to get the truth about the boat trip from him. Later, Harry turns the tables and forces the Police Captain (Dan Seymour) to release Eddie and to hand over signed exit passes, so that the Bursacs, Eddie, Marie and he can leave the island.

THE SPEECH

The scene between Harry and Marie (who is trying to seduce) him is powerful, sexy and inspirational at the same time:

> "Who was the girl, Steve? ... The one that left you with such a high opinion of women? She must have been quite a gal. You think I lied to you about this, don't you? Well, it just happens there's thirty-odd dollars here. Not enough for boat fare, or any other kind of fare. Just enough for me to say 'no' if I feel like it, and you can have it if you want it ... You wouldn't take anything from anybody would you? ... You know Steve, you're not very hard to figure. Only at times. Sometimes I know exactly what you're going to say. Most of the time. The other times, the other times you're just a stinker." She kisses him a second time and, not getting much response, breathes, as she leaves the room, "It's even better when you help ... Uh, sure you won't change your mind about this? ... This belongs to me and so do my lips, I don't see any difference ... Okay … you don't have to do anything. Not with me. Oh, maybe just whistle. You remember how to whistle, don't you? Just put your lips together ... and blow."

Our hero remains in his chair, smoking a cigarette. After she has left, he makes the sound of a cat-call whistle and then chuckles the Bogey chuckle to himself. This speech is pivotal to the film and the chemistry between the two main characters is fizzing.

FROM THE FILM

15 IT'S A WONDERFUL LIFE

DIRECTED BY FRANK CAPRA (1946)

This is one of the most warming and positive films made by director Frank Capra. It was his own personal favourite as it was James Stewart's, although it flopped financially on release. It only became *the* Christmas movie in and from the 1970s when TV channels could air it for nothing after its copyright lapsed. The screenplay was based on *The Greatest Gift*, an original short story first written on a Christmas card by Philip Van Doren Stern.

THE STORY

On Christmas Eve in Bedford Falls, a guardian angel, Clarence, is assigned to convince the desperate George Bailey not to commit suicide. George is a good man who has sacrificed his dreams and youth on behalf of the citizens of his small town. He inherited his father's financial business and didn't travel the world or go to university as planned because he felt obliged to stay and help the unfortunate folk of the town. George resists the proposals of the evil banker Mr. Potter (who has renamed Bedford Falls Pottersville) and, in order to protect the poor community, George doesn't sell his loan business.

George marries his beloved Mary Hatch Bailey and they have four children, but life is tough. There's a big hole in the accounts – caused by his uncle Billy and the nasty Mr. Potter – to the tune of eight thousand dollars. George has had enough and decides to commit suicide since he believes he's worth more dead than alive. When Clarence realises he can't convince George to live, he decides to show our protagonist what life in town would have been like if he had never existed. We see a nightmarish vision of darkness and corruption and even his mother, whom we know as a kindly soul in the rest of the film, now appears hard-bitten and cruel – and refuses to recognise George in a scene that dramatises the identity crisis that's at the heart of the movie. George is heartened and concludes that life is after all wonderful.

THE SPEECH

In a meeting of the board of the Bailey Building and Loan Company that gathers to vote on its future, Mr. Potter (Lionel Barrymore) believes that the loan policies of George's company only produce: "a discontented, lazy rabble instead of a thrifty working class". George's defence of his dead father's name to Mr. Potter, in an address to the Loan Board, is a wonderful and optimistic moment.

"... Just remember this, Mr. Potter, that this rabble you're talking about, they do most of the working and paying and living and dying in this community. Well, is it too much to have them work and pay and live and die in a couple of decent rooms and a bath? Anyway, my father didn't think so. People were human beings to him, but to you, a warped, frustrated old man, they're cattle. Well, in my book he died a much richer man than you'll ever be ... I know very well what you're talking about. You're talking about something you can't get your fingers on, and it's galling you. That's what you're talking about, I know. Well ... I've said too much. I – You're the Board here. You do what you want with this thing. There's just one thing more, though. This town needs this measly one-horse institution if only to have some place where people can come without crawling to Potter."

The speech is soaring hope incarnate and we see a light at the end of a dark tunnel.

FROM THE PLAY

16 A STREETCAR NAMED DESIRE

WRITTEN BY TENESSEE WILLIAMS (1947)

This play won the Pulitzer Prize for drama in 1948. The London production opened in 1949, directed by Laurence Olivier. In 1951 a film version starring Marlon Brando, Jessica Tandy, Kim Hunter and Karl Malden and directed by Elia Kazan won four Academy Awards. Allan Grey is a homosexual character in the play who (away from the onstage story) has committed suicide. Because of the Hays Code (which dictated what was acceptable and what not from 1930 right up to 1968), the reason for his suicide had to be changed to a general "weakness".

Blanche Dubois' explanation of her route in the play is terrific: "They told me to take a streetcar named Desire, transfer to one called Cemeteries and ride six blocks and get off at – Elysian Fields!" Greek mythology has it that The Elysian Fields were the final resting places of the souls of the brave and the virtuous.

THE STORY

World War II has recently ended and Blanche Dubois arrives from Mississippi to visit her sister, Stella, who lives in a shabby apartment building in a poor district of New Orleans. The sisters actually come from southern aristocratic stock. Stella moved to New Orleans while Blanche managed the homestead, became a successful English teacher and married Allen Grey whom she idolised. But her world fell to bits when she discovered that her husband was having a homosexual affair. Disgraced, he killed himself. Blanche then had many flings with many men, including a 17-year-old student; the powers that be at the school in which she taught found out and she lost her job. Creditors seized the family home when she could not pay for its upkeep.

In New Orleans, she stays with Stella and Stella's crude, outspoken, poker-playing and violent husband, Stanley Kowalski. Though bitter, somewhat beaten by her past and prone to drink, Blanche does her best, even lying when necessary (and therefore often), to keep up appearances. Blanche gets on with one of Stanley's gambling friends, Mitch, but Stanley poisons him against her. Stanley and Blanche loathe each other. The dramatic tension of the play reaches its height when Stanley rapes Blanche which tips her over the edge into insanity. She is committed to a mental institution.

THE SPEECH

At the play's start, Blanche is immediately on the defensive as she describes how hard she has worked to keep the family plantation running while Stella went off to live in New Orleans. In narrating what happened to her husband, their parents and the homestead, Blanche becomes angry – angry that she had to manage the sick and dying, angry at the loss of her husband, income and the family home. On one level, Blanche craves pity. On another level, she keeps going, showing a flawed, inspirational stoicism:

“I took the blows on my face and my body! All those deaths! The long parade to the graveyard. Father, Mother … You came just in time for funerals Stella. And funerals are pretty compared to death. Funerals are quiet, but deaths not always. Sometimes their breathing is hoarse, sometimes it rattles, sometimes they cry out to you, "Don't let me go!" … I saw! Saw! And now you sit there telling me with your eyes that I let the place go. How in hell do you think all that sickness and dying was paid for? Death is expensive Miss Stella! … The Grim Reaper put his tent up on our doorstep! … That was it Stella! … Yes, accuse me! Sit there and stare at me, thinking I let the place go. I let the place go! Where were you Stella? In bed with your Polack!”

FROM THE FILM AND PLAY

17 HAMLET

WRITTEN BY SHAKESPEARE (1602)

Shakespeare is a passion of mine and *Hamlet* is one of my favourite plays. The film (1948) was adapted and directed by Laurence Olivier, who also played the lead. In 1990, Ian Charleson played the part on the London stage beautifully, not long before he died. Some say Charleson's Hamlet was the best ever. In film, Zeffirelli provided a version in 1990 and Kenneth Branagh another in 1996. It's a play that's on somewhere in the world at any one time.

Hamlet is also probably the most famous play in the English language. Shakespeare achieved mastery in his craft and maturity in this work through the brilliant depiction of a man's struggle with two opposing forces: moral integrity and the need to avenge his father's murder. The Act 1, scene 3 speech, "to be, or not to be", is the most famous of soliloquies.

Olivier's film won two Academy Awards for Best Actor and Best Picture.

THE STORY

Prince Hamlet (Laurence Olivier) mourns his father's death and is distressed over the subsequent and speedy marriage of his mother, Queen Gertrude (Eileen Herlie), to Claudius (Basil Sydney), Hamlet's uncle. The ghost of Hamlet's father appears to the young prince and tells him that he, Hamlet's father, was poisoned by Claudius, Hamlet's uncle (now married to Hamlet's mother, Gertrude). Hamlet swears revenge. He kills the eavesdropping Polonius (Felix Aylmer), the court chamberlain. Polonius's daughter, Ophelia (Jean Simmons), loves the Prince, but his behaviour drives her to madness and she dies by drowning, probably suicide. Polonius' son, Laertes (Terence Morgan) returns to Denmark to avenge his father's death and that of his sister. A duel takes place and ends with the deaths of Gertrude, Laertes, Claudius and Hamlet.

THE SPEECH

The "to be or not to be" soliloquy is a brilliant example of Shakespeare's ability to express a character's torment. The soliloquy is written in iambic pentameter with a feminine ending, meaning that each line has eleven syllables rather than ten, the last of which is unstressed. The speech is inspirational because it is not definitive about accepting death and despondency, but allows for hope and resolution, although Hamlet doesn't conclude how. The soliloquy goes a long way to make us realise that *our* problems are small.

Hamlet is confused and unhappy and lists life's many torments. On the other hand, he is unsure what death may bring.

His sanity is beginning to unravel, or at least, this is what the audience is led to believe. Whether or not Hamlet is feigning madness is still hotly debated. If the language alone is inspirational, the thought process is inspiration on fire.

"To be, or not to be: that is the question:

Whether 'tis nobler in the mind to suffer
The slings and arrows of outrageous fortune,
Or to take arms against a sea of troubles,
And by opposing end them?
To die: to sleep;
No more; and by a sleep to say we end
The heart-ache and the thousand natural shocks
That flesh is heir to, 'tis a consummation
Devoutly to be wish'd. To die, to sleep;
To sleep: perchance to dream: ay, there's the rub;
For in that sleep of death what dreams may come
When we have shuffled off this mortal coil,
Must give us pause: there's the respect
That makes calamity of so long life;
For who would bear the whips and scorns of time,
The oppressor's wrong, the proud man's contumely,
The pangs of despised love, the law's delay,
The insolence of office and the spurns
That patient merit of the unworthy takes,
When he himself might his quietus make
With a bare bodkin? who would fardels bear,
To grunt and sweat under a weary life,
But that the dread of something after death,
The undiscover'd country from whose bourn
No traveller returns, puzzles the will
And makes us rather bear those ills we have
Than fly to others that we know not of?
Thus conscience does make cowards of us all;
And thus the native hue of resolution
Is sicklied o'er with the pale cast of thought,
And enterprises of great pith and moment
With this regard their currents turn awry,
And lose the name of action ... ”

FROM THE FILM

18 ALL THE KING'S MEN

DIRECTED BY ROBERT ROSSEN (1945)

This is a story about the rise and fall of Huey Pierce Long, Louisiana's colourful state governor and Democratic US Senator (1932-35). It's a tale about the corruption of power and how power corrupts. It's also about a man who becomes just like the sleazy politicians whom he has criticised and vilified. The film was adapted and based on the Pulitzer Prize-winning and best-selling 1946 novel of the same name by Robert Penn Warren. Broderick Crawford as Willie Stark gives an impressive performance as he is transformed from a pleasant, honest and naive lawyer into an unscrupulous and unpleasant politician. The film won three Academy Awards: Best Actor for Crawford, Best Supporting Actress for Mercedes McCambridge (in her screen debut) and overall Best Picture.

The film was remade with the same title in 2006, directed by Steven Zaillian and starring Sean Penn as Willie Stark (Broderick's role), Jude Law, Kate Winslet, Mark Ruffalo and Patricia Clarkson. It wasn't a success.

THE STORY

In his rise to become governor of his state, cheerful lawyer Willie Stark loses his political innocence and becomes just as corrupt as the politicians he once fought. In the process, he ruins the lives of his family and colleagues. The plot is a thinly disguised version of the rise and assassination of real-life 1930s Louisiana Governor, Huey Long. The film posits the notion of whether an end always justifies the means. Many of Stark's objectives are certainly intended well, but he reaches these goals through guile and corruption. When Stark's son, Tom (John Derek), kills a passenger in a drunk-driving incident and is paralysed in the process, Stark discovers that not everyone can be bought off and his corrupt career falters. Watch the movie. Listen to the whole speech. The rhetoric is outstanding – even though we know that the corruption is deep-set. Rhetoric, even with false motive, superbly crafted and superbly delivered can convert listeners and can, of course, inspire – as history shows us only too well.

THE SPEECH

Willie Stark makes a rousing, slightly inebriated campaign speech at a barbecue that purports to set out his supposed stance on political help for the downtrodden. It pulls us in and it *does* inspire.

> "My friends. I have a speech here. It's a speech about what this state needs. There's no need in my telling you what this state needs. You are the state and you know what you need. You over there, look at your pants. Have they got holes in the knees? … And you, what about your kids? Are they growing up ignorant as dirt, ignorant as you 'cause there's no school for 'em? No, I'm not gonna read you any speech. But I am gonna tell you a story … I'm going to stay in this race. I'm on my own and I'm out for blood …

AN OVERVIEW OF

CHAPTER TWO

Dominated by World War II, the decade was a time for introspection and disillusionment. Tennessee Williams wrote of disillusionment and futility in *The Glass Menagerie* and *A Streetcar Named Desire*. But there were also lighter moments, including a rebirth of musical theatre notably in *Oklahoma!* And there was an outpouring of good films and plays. Most American and British film plots had a fairly narrow and predictable set of morals and, if German or Japanese characters were included, they were one-dimensional villains.

The story of the Joad family in *The Grapes of Wrath* captured a turbulent moment of broader villainy and depression in American history and fired up vast numbers of people both via the Steinbeck novel and the film. In writing his novel, Steinbeck attempted not only to describe the plight of migrant workers during the Depression, but also to offer a pointed criticism of the policies that had caused that plight in the first place. Through the characters we learn of universal ideals and struggles, not only specific ones. Steinbeck consistently points to the fact that the migrants' great suffering is caused not by bad weather or mere misfortune, but by their fellow human beings. *Mrs. Miniver* looks at hurt and harm, grief and injustice in a different way – no less moving. It was the top-grossing film of 1942 and the second biggest box-office hit of the decade, after *Gone With the Wind. Casablanca* grows more legendary as time goes by for, like all legends, it remains exceptional and inimitable. It is a basic story about good versus evil in the most difficult of times. This is a simple tale that explores (and then resolves) the inner struggles of ordinary people who fight not only against immense evil, but also against their own inner demons and conflicting emotions.

Oklahoma! shows us something of comfort and satisfaction. Again, there's the integral good versus bad story mixed with the celebration of beauty and relationships. Songs such as *Oh, What a Beautiful Mornin'* are iconic – and no less inspirational than any speech.

The idea conveyed in *The Glass Menagerie* is that of image versus reality. Amanda has a picture of the world and of gentlemen callers, but that isn't a reality in the St. Louis ghetto. Laura has her own imaginary reality. Tom tries to escape a reality and eventually does so in his father's footsteps. We are left with a sadness certainly, but also a sense of hope in Tom's (and, indeed, our) future.

Understanding goodness is a big theme in the world of film and plays. The reason *It's A Wonderful Life* has had such enduring popularity is that it shows what can be the value of a single individual and the contribution to the greater good he or she can make. George Bailey, as brilliantly portrayed by James Stewart, is the kind of ordinary hero with whom we can all identify.

Two of the most important names of 20th century theatre are Eugene O'Neill and Tennessee Williams. Both pushed the exploration of the human soul to the very limit. Drama will never be the same because of the work of these two men. *A Streetcar Named Desire* makes us think. It makes us pity Blanche, hate Stanley, wonder what's really wrong with Stella and half hate, half pity Mitch. The ending is sad and shocking, particularly when Mitch sees Blanche, crumpled and writhing on the floor and he hits Stanley, screaming "You did this to her!" The passion and feeling of loss promote a sense of awe. *Hamlet* is awesome too – for its language, its character analysis, its portrayal of a tormented soul. Here is a young man whose speech contains the ingredients of melancholy mixed with indignation. The moral of the story is that nothing good can come of going against good conscience. Hamlet endures as the object of universal identification because his central moral dilemma transcends the Elizabethan period and applies now as much as it did then.

Chapter Three

THE 1950s

"A career is wonderful thing, but you can't snuggle up to it on a cold night." Marilyn Monroe

From the film *High Noon* (1952), where Marshall Will Kane (Gary Cooper) says to Deputy Sheriff Harvey Pell (Lloyd Bridges): "Don't shove me Harv. I'm tired of being shoved."

This decade was known for post-war affluence and consumerism. There was increased choice of leisure time activities, conformity, the Korean War, middle-class values, the rise of rock and roll and the spread of fast food restaurants. There was a baby boom, electric appliances in the home became the norm, white racist terrorism emerged in America and abstract art blossomed. The first credit card (Diners Club) was launched in 1951. The spiral structure of DNA was discovered in 1953 and a vaccine was produced against polio in 1955.

Both the East and West had nuclear weapons. The Cold War, predominantly between the Soviet Union and the US, became a reality. The first satellite to orbit the earth, Sputnik 1, was launched by the Soviet Union in 1957. The Soviet Union also built the first nuclear power-plant. West Germany picked itself up and, via the establishment of the EEC, enjoyed a period of huge growth. Japan grew too, particularly in the supply of electronics. There were hot spots in the world, not least in the Middle East. The Suez Crisis of 1956 brought the world once more to the brink of wider conflict when the passage of oil through the Suez Canal was blocked.

In 1950 Ray Bradbury published *The Martian Chronicles* and J.D. Salinger's *The Catcher in the Rye* came out in 1951. Vladimir Nabokov's *Lolita* drew mixed response and absolute moral outrage from some quarters and in 1955, Tolkein gave us *The Return of the King*, the final part of his famous trilogy. Jack Kerouac published *On the Road* in 1957, Leon Uris produced *Exodus* the next year and Günter Grass delivered *The Tin Drum* in 1959.

Gigi (1951) was a popular Broadway play based on Colette's 1945 novel of the same name, starring Audrey Hepburn in the title role. *The Mousetrap* is an Agatha Christie murder mystery play which opened in the West End of London in 1952 and has been running continuously there since. Arthur Miller wrote the play *The Crucible* (1953) as an allegory to McCarthyism, Samuel Beckett came out with *Waiting for Godot* (also in 1953) and Tennessee Williams' *Cat on a Hot Tin Roof* won a Pulitzer Prize in 1955. Europe began to produce a wave of films in the 1950s. In Italy, Federico Fellini delivered *La Strada* (1954) and *Nights of Cabiria* (1957), both of which won Academy Awards. Swedish director Ingmar Bergman made *Smiles of a Summer Night* (1955), *The Seventh Seal* (1957) and *Wild Strawberries* (also 1957). Jean Cocteau offered *Orphée* (1950).

The late 1940s and 1950s also saw the rise of the anti-heroes such as James Dean, Paul Newman and Marlon Brando. One of the most popular films was Leo McCarey's romantic drama *An Affair to Remember* (1957), a remake of the director's own powerfully moving film, *Love Affair* (1939). The same story was later to form the framework of Nora Ephron's warm *Sleepless in Seattle* (1993).

The decade saw the rise of rock 'n' roll and a new teenage market. Many adults regarded the new generation with suspicion and there were several films about rebellious and often cruel teenagers. *The Wild One* (1954), directed by Laslo Benedek, was so shocking to some that it was banned in the UK until the 1960s.

James Dean was the epitome of adolescent pain, appearing in only three films before his death in 1955. His first starring role was in Elia Kazan's *East of Eden* (1955), followed the same year by Nicholas Ray's *Rebel Without a Cause* and then George Stevens' epic saga *Giant* (1956). Of course, this was also Elvis Presley's decade and he made his first record, *That's All Right Mama,* in 1954.

Two films based on Jules Verne's novels were produced: Disney's adventure story *20,000 Leagues Under the Sea* (1954) and *Journey to the Centre of the Earth* (1959). David Lean's *The Bridge on the River Kwai* (1957) was a big-budget epic and William Wyler directed the award-winning remake of *Ben-Hur (*1959).

Marilyn Monroe hit the screens with a punch. Director Joseph L. Mankiewicz created *All About Eve (*1950), which received six Academy Awards and starred Monroe as an aspiring starlet and Bette Davis as ageing theatre star.

World War II movies this decade included *The Caine Mutiny* (1954), adapted from Herman Wouk's unputdownable novel, with a brilliant Humphrey Bogart on trial as the mad but fascinating Lt. Commander Queeg. And there was the story of a young Dutch girl in hiding before being betrayed, discovered and sent to a concentration camp – *The Diary of Anne Frank (1959)*, directed by George Stevens.

The decade also witnessed the prodigious rise of great musicals such as *Annie Get Your Gun* (1950), *Singin' in the Rain* (1952) and *Showboat* (1951) with the unforgettable rendition of *Ol' Man River* by William Warfield. *Kiss Me Kate* (1953) was a play within a play and a musical version of Shakespeare's *The Taming of the Shrew* and *The King and I* (1956) was the filmic version of the Rodgers and Hammerstein 1951 Broadway musical hit.

From Here to Eternity (1953) was considered immoral by many – partly due to that well publicised on-the-beach scene. And *Cat on a Hot Tin Roof* (1958), directed by Richard Brooks, was regarded by some as too much with its sexual references. *Death of a Salesman (*1951) was a screen adaptation of Arthur Miller's Pulitzer Prize-winning play. And there was the brilliant, thought-provoking, grim, anti-nuclear film, *On the Beach* (1959), a doomsday account (based on the great Nevil Shute's novel) of an odd mix of survivors in the aftermath of a nuclear attack, with Gregory Peck as an inspirational submarine commander.

Darryl Zanuck's *Island in the Sun* (1957) was daring for its time, since the Hays Code banned miscegenation. It offered two interracial romances between John Justin and Dorothy Dandridge and Harry Belafonte and Joan Fontaine. The film presented the first scene in an American film where a white woman was kissed by an Afro-American man.

Perhaps the most famous Western of all then or actually since was Fred Zinnemann's *High Noon* (1952), for which Gary Cooper won a Best Actor Academy Award. From Japanese director Akira Kurosawa came a terrific film, *The Seven Samurai* (1954) – a 16th century story about seven hired professionals commissioned to defend a small farming village.

Science fiction raised its head – Robert Wise directed the classic *The Day the Earth Stood Still* (1951) and Byron Haskin directed *The War of the Worlds* (1953) adapted from H.G. Wells' 1898 book. The UK's Hammer Studios' low-budget series of horror films featured some great results, such as *The Curse of Frankenstein* (1957) directed by Terence Fisher.

There were some other magic moments, many inspirational. Disney delivered *Cinderella (*1950), *Alice in Wonderland* (1951), *Peter Pan* (1953), *Lady and the Tramp* (1955) and *Sleeping Beauty* (1959). John Osborne's "angry young man" play, *Look Back in Anger,* was brought to the screen by director Tony Richardson in 1959, starring Richard Burton. Billy Wilder directed *The Seven Year Itch* (1955) with Marilyn Monroe's famous scene above a subway grating. Hitchcock directed the classic *Rear Window* (1954) with James Stewart and the beautiful Grace Kelly, *North by Northwest* (1959) and *Vertigo* (1958). Phew.

FROM THE FILM

19 THE BROWNING VERSION

DIRECTED BY ANTHONY ASQUITH (1951)

This film starred Michael Redgrave and is based upon the 1948 play of the same name by Terence Rattigan who also wrote the screenplay. Michael Redgrave won Best Actor and Terrence Rattigan won Best Screenplay at the Cannes Film Festival.

THE STORY

Andrew Crocker-Harris (Michael Redgrave) is suffering from ill health and nearing retirement as an English public school Classics teacher. The film focuses on his final few days at the school, during which he feels he has failed as a teacher, something underlined by the infidelity of his wife Millie (Jean Kent) and his sudden understanding that the pupils loathe him. The sensitivity of one pupil, Taplow (Brian Smith), breaks through Crocker-Harris' reserved British exterior. The title of the play refers to a gift from Taplow – Robert Browning's translation of the Agamemnon. Taplow has inscribed the book with a Greek phrase the translation of which reads: "God from afar looks graciously upon a gentle master."

However, it takes the final departure of Millie, just before the school's graduation ceremony, to wake Crocker-Harris up once and for all. He discards his prepared speech and speaks openly to the assembled students, delivering a moving apology for having failed them as their teacher.

THE SPEECH

The film is an emotionally wrenching exploration of a defeated failure, but which ultimately (and surprisingly) becomes uplifting; it inspires Crocker-Harris' audience (and us) through the catharsis it evokes. Redgrave is nothing short of sensational, grabbing the viewer with a quiet intensity that is all the more remarkable considering that the character's inner passion is buried so far deep inside him.

As Crocker-Harris prepares to speak to the school, he discards his prepared speech, having lost his wife, his job and, really, his life:

"You must excuse me. I had prepared a speech, but I find now that I have nothing to say. Or rather, I have three very small words, but they are most deeply felt. They are these: I am sorry. I am sorry because I have failed to give you what you had the right to demand of me as your teacher: sympathy, encouragement and humanity … I claim no excuses. When I came here, I – I knew what I had to do and I have not done it. I have failed … miserably failed. But I can only hope that you and the countless others who have gone before will find it in your hearts to forgive me for having let you down. I shall not find it so easy to forgive myself …"

FROM THE FILM

20 DEATH OF A SALESMAN

DIRECTED BY LÁSZLÓ BENEDEK (1951)

Adapted from the play of the same name by Arthur Miller, this film was a box office failure mostly because the subject matter (the failure of the American dream) didn't appeal. The play, which made its debut in 1949, remains one of the most popular of the twentieth century. In its first production directed by Elia Kazan and starring Lee. J. Cobb, it ran for 745 performances and won a Pulitzer Prize.

THE STORY

Willy Loman (Frederic March), a sixty-year-old travelling salesman, can't keep his mind on the present. He keeps drifting back and forth between reality and memory, looking for precisely where his life has gone wrong. He's been demoted to a commission-only salesman, which is where he was at the start of his career. He has always believed that being well-liked was the key to success.

Throughout his life, Willy has also attempted to show his sons the keys to success and to prepare them, or at least Biff, his oldest son (Kevin McCarthy), for excellence in the business world. Willy always pretended to be an important, respected and successful salesman in order to win the love and respect of his family. When reality hits him and destroys the image he has been promoting, his whole life begins to collapse. Not only that, he realises he has taught his sons the wrong lessons of life.

Unemployed, destitute and broken, Willy wants to prove, mostly to Biff, that his life hasn't been a waste of time. He thinks he'll be of more value to his family dead so Biff can start his own business with the life insurance money. He commits suicide. Willy's long-suffering wife, Linda (Mildred Dunnock), believes that all debts are now clear and that the family might have a little money. However, the insurance policy doesn't cover suicide; only Willy's family and their two neighbours attend the funeral.

THE SPEECH

This speech is inspirational because we want it to be. We want it to be true even though we know it isn't. We want there to be hope. This is pathos at its best and its stab is all the more hurtful because of the power of its words. What's more, most of us can empathise with the Loman character. When we watch the film and play (superbly produced of course), we are there.

Willy is deluded in thinking that looks are all his sons Biff and Happy will need to get ahead:

“That's just what I mean, Bernard can get the best marks in school, y'understand, but when he gets out in the business world, y'understand, you are going to be five times ahead of him. That's why I thank Almighty God you're both built like Adonises. Because the man who makes an appearance in the business world, the man who creates personal interest, is the man who gets ahead. Be liked and you will never want. You take me for instance, I never have to wait in line to see a buyer. 'Willy Loman is here!' That's all they have to know, and I go right through ...”

FROM THE FILM

21 ON THE WATERFRONT

DIRECTED BY ELIA KAZAN (1954)

The film, with a score by Leonard Bernstein, is a classic, award-winning and, back then, highly controversial gangster drama. This is New York's dock workers' struggle for work and dignity under the heavy and unrelenting pressure of very tough unions that would resort to anything to get their own way. The film won eight Academy Awards.

THE STORY

Terry Malloy (Marlon Brando) wants to become a boxer, but all he can do is dream. He tends his pigeons and is an occasional runner at the docks for Johnny Friendly (Lee J. Cobb), the corrupt boss of the dockers union who runs rackets and extortion. Terry, who's not particularly sharp, is used to lure a popular dockworker out to an ambush so he can be killed by Friendly's thugs. Later Terry meets the dead man's sister, Edie (Eva Marie Saint), and feels responsible for the man's death. She introduces him to Father Barry (Karl Malden), who urges Terry to give information to the police that will finish the dock racketeers, in particular Friendly, for good.

Terry is torn. He's also fallen for Edie. Both Edie and Father Barry urge Terry to testify. Another dockworker, Timothy (K.O.) Dugan (Pat Henning), agrees to testify after Father Barry's promise of unwavering support. However Dugan is crushed by crates of whiskey in a so-called accident. Distressed by what he sees happening around him, Terry wants to testify. Friendly decides he must be disposed of unless Charley (Terry's brother), a successful union organiser, can keep him quiet. Charley tries to bribe Terry with the offer a terrific job and finally threatens him, but sees that Terry is adamant about testifying.

Terry places the blame for his own downward spiral on successful, but crooked, Charley. In one of the most powerful scenes in film history, Terry tells Charley that "I coulda been a contender". Charley urges Terry to get far away from the docks and New York and gives him a gun. However, Friendly learns of this and has Charley brutally murdered. Terry sets out to shoot Friendly, but Father Barry convinces him that the best way to beat Friendly is by testifying.

Terry gets to fight Friendly and, while he gains the initial upper hand in a vicious brawl, he's eventually severely beaten by Friendly and his thugs. The dockworkers declare huge support for Terry and only go back to work when Terry testifies against Friendly and the union.

THE SPEECH

Terry is trying to explain to Charley what's gone wrong in his (Terry's) life. He blames his brother for his own failure. He knows that there was a point when he could have won, could have achieved something through his skill as a boxer. They're in the back of a cab:

“It wasn't him, Charley! It was you. You remember that night in the Garden, you came down to my dressing room and said: 'Kid, this ain't your night. We're going for the price on Wilson.' You remember that? 'This ain't your night!' … I coulda taken Wilson apart! So what happens? He gets the title shot outdoors in the ball park – and whadda I get? A one-way ticket to Palookaville ... You was my brother, Charley. You shoulda looked out for me a little bit. You shoulda taken care of me – just a little bit – so I wouldn't have to take them dives for the short-end money … I coulda had class. I coulda been a contender. I coulda been somebody, instead of a bum ... It was you, Charley.”

The speech, sometimes quiet, sometimes loud and desperate, has huge power and weight. We can feel the frustration and angst, the hurt and the loss. We can also recognise, along with Terry, what might have been and that's inspirational indeed.

FROM THE FILM

22 EAST OF EDEN

DIRECTED BY ELIA KAZAN (1955)

The film, an adaptation of John Steinbeck's novel (1952), is Kazan's version of the Biblical story of rival brothers, Cain and Abel – and has the perennial theme of a lost dream. It starred James Dean and Jo Van Fleet, who won Best Supporting Actress Academy Award.

THE STORY

Set in 1917 and just before America joined World War I, the story revolves around Adam Trask (Raymond Massey) and his two sons, Cal (James Dean) and Aron (Richard Davalos). Adam is stern, tough, religious, self-righteous and always looks sour. He's a lettuce farmer in Salinas, California, held in high esteem by the local community. Cal and Aron are led to believe that their mother died some time ago, but Cal discovers that she (Jo Van Fleet) owns a brothel in the nearby town.

Cal is jealous of the love and attention his brother Aron receives from their father, although on the surface it seems he couldn't care less about anything. There is a celebrated scene where Cal's birthday present for his father is rejected and the young man's hurt is so palpable that he delivers a moan of utter anguish.

In Cal's mind, the only way to earn his father's respect and love is by setting up a business venture that would compensate his father's recent business losses. To do so, he has to borrow money from his mother and invests it in beans, a lucrative venture in wartime.

Cal's business does well and he decides to give some money to his father at a surprise birthday party. As this gets underway, Aron suddenly announces that he and Abra are engaged. While Adam is openly pleased, both Abra and Cal, who are attracted to each other, are uneasy. Cal gives the money to his father, but Adam refuses it, considering it to be earned by war profiteering. Cal is dumbfounded and leaves the room. Abra goes after him to console him; Aron follows and warns Cal to stay away from her. This is all too much for Cal, so he takes the smug, self-righteous Aron to see their mother.

The shock of seeing their mother running a whore house drives Aron to drink and, to escape, he enlists in the army. Adam rushes to the station to stop him, but can't. Adam then suffers a stroke which leaves him paralysed and unable to talk. A nurse is employed to look after him. Cal tries to talk to his dad, but gets no response. Abra pleads with Adam to show Cal some love and Cal makes a last bid for acceptance. His father manages to speak. He insists that his son get rid of the nurse and demands that Cal stay. At the end of the film we see Cal sitting by his father, both alone, but beginning (we like to think) to come together.

THE SPEECH

Abra is talking to the incapacitated Adam Trask, who's just suffered a stroke, regarding his relationship with Cal. It's a short speech, but enormously powerful and certainly inspirational. Here is a desperate moment, a plea for a father to love his son, a son to whom he's shown little fondness. It's inspirational because we hope that it might at last make a difference.

> “Mr. Trask, it's awful not to be loved. It's the worst thing in the world. Don't ask me – even if you could – how I know that. I just know it. It makes you mean, and violent, and cruel. And that's the way Cal has always felt, Mr. Trask. All his life! Maybe you didn't mean it that way – but it's true. You never gave him your love. You never asked for his. You never asked him for one thing.”

There's another line of Abra's which adds value to the above and makes one believe that at some point Adam Trask might find space in his heart for Cal:

> “But you must give him some sign, Mr. Trask, some sign that you love him ... or he'll never be a man. All his life he'll feel guilty and alone unless you release him.”

FROM THE FILM

23 MOBY DICK

DIRECTED BY JOHN HUSTON (1956)

Herman Melville's brilliant novel, *Moby Dick*, on which the film is based, was published in 1851. It explores a wide variety of ideas, including views on American society, philosophy, class, religion, God and the devil. The 1956 film is one of the better known adaptations of the book and perhaps the best remembered version.

THE STORY

Ishmael (Richard Baseheart), a young seaman and the story's narrator, joins a whaling ship, the *Pequod,* along with a fellow seaman, Queequeg (Friedrich von Ledebur). The *Pequod* is covered with the teeth of sperm whales and is captained by Ahab (Gregory Peck), who has lost a leg to a sperm whale and now has a false leg made from a sperm whale's jaw. Ahab tells his crew of his ambition to kill Moby Dick, a great white whale and, according to the captain, the embodiment of evil.

The ship meets another, on board of which is a mad prophet, who predicts ruin for anyone trying to harm Moby Dick. There seems to be some truth in this because several nasty accidents occur to Ahab's crew. A typhoon hits the *Pequod* which is then struck by lightning, something that Ahab considers a sign of impending success rather than doom. The first mate thinks this is nonsense and considers killing Ahab. After the storm ends, one of the sailors falls from one of the ship's masts and drowns. The ship meets more whaling vessels, each of which has had bad encounters with Moby Dick.

Ahab finally sights the great whale and the harpoon boats are launched. Moby Dick attacks Ahab's small boat, destroying it. The next day, the whale is sighted again and the boats are lowered once more. The whale is harpooned, but again it attacks Ahab's harpoon boat. On the third day, the boats again go after Moby Dick, which attacks them, rams the *Pequod* and sinks it. Ahab is then caught in a harpoon line and hurled out of his boat to his death. All the remaining whaleboats and men are caught in the vortex created by the sinking ship and are drowned. Ishmael escapes and is eventually rescued.

THE SPEECH

Despite the fear of damnation implicit in a sermon delivered by Father Mapple (Orson Welles), warning that those who challenge the sea could lose their souls, Ishmael signs on to join the *Pequod.* Father Mapple was once a sailor and a harpooner, but has dedicated his life to the church. He has a reputation for sincerity, so Ishmael cannot suspect him of any trickery in what he says.

The sermon is stirring and inspirational – predominantly focusing on the forces of good battling those of evil. Father Mapple describes the soul of man and the need to keep the forces of good onside lest temptation and the devil beat you. He uses Jonah and the whale as his theme, for Jonah is disobedient to God. Father Mapple recounts the terrors in Jonah's soul. The lesson of Jonah is to preach the truth in the face of falsehood, even if this truth may be appalling:

“... Jonah did the Almighty's bidding. And what was that, shipmates? To preach the truth in the face of falsehood! Now shipmates, woe to him who seeks to pour oil on the troubled waters when God has brewed them into a gale. Yea, woe to him who, as the Pilot Paul has it, while preaching to others is himself a castaway. But delight is to him who against the proud gods and commodores of this earth stands forth his own inexorable self, who destroys all sin, though he pluck it out from the robes of senators and judges! And Eternal Delight shall be his, who coming to lay him down can say: 'O Father, mortal or immortal, here I die. I have driven to be thine, more than to be this world's or mine own, yet this is nothing I leave eternity to Thee.' For what is man that he should live out the lifetime of his God?”

The instruction is strong: with truth there is redemption. With redemption, there is hope, inspiration.

FROM THE FILM

24 PATHS OF GLORY

DIRECTED BY STANLEY KUBRICK (1957)

This war film is essentially anti-war, has been seen as anti-French and was indeed banned in France until 1975. Others say that it's bang on the money and that incidents much like those portrayed in the film certainly took place in all areas of conflict during World War I.

THE STORY

In 1917, the pompous and immoral French General Broulard (Adolphe Menjou) orders his troops to seize the heavily fortified Ant Hill from the Germans. General Mireau (George MacReady) knows this action to be suicidal, but for his own ambition he will sacrifice his men without qualms. Colonel Dax (Kirk Douglas) knows that the mission is foolish, but following orders, leads the charge resulting in huge losses. After witnessing the slaughter of their comrades, many of the French troops refuse to leave the trenches. Mireau wants his artillery to fire on his own soldiers (but the artillery does not). He convinces himself that the failure of the action was due to the cowardice of his men and thinks that, for the sake of appearances and discipline, three soldiers must be chosen to be executed as an example.

Colonel Dax (a lawyer in civilian life) defends the three and pleads for their lives, but to no avail. Last minute evidence proves that Mireau was and is incompetent, but that too is ignored by the gutless Broulard. The three condemned men are killed by firing squad. Following this, Broulard makes it clear that Mireau will be investigated for the order to fire artillery on his own men and but instead offers Dax Mireau's position, insinuating that Dax had been angling for promotion all along. Dax is furious and turns it down, making the cynical Broulard see him as a fool.

Meanwhile some of Dax's soldiers are in a tavern when the proprietor brings a young captured German woman (Christane Kubrick) on stage and makes her sing the German folk song, *The Faithful Hussar*. Touched by her song, the hardened troops end up humming along, some openly weeping. Dax overhears this scene from outside. He is given orders that the regiment must return to the front (and certain doom), but Dax wants to give them a few minutes more.

THE SPEECH

The ballad sung by the captured German girl touches the French soldiers. The scene ends with Commander Dax giving his weary men the brief rest that they were promised:

"Well, give the men a few minutes more, Sergeant," he says, as we hear drums and military music playing the song, *Soldier Boy*, rising in volume and drowning out the sound of the folk song. This is only one line, but it has enormous inspiration and pathos built in. It ensures that the weight of man's strange inhumanity to man (on all levels), of greed, of senseless waste – does not go without notice, even if that notice is small.

AN OVERVIEW OF CHAPTER THREE

Death Of A Salesman is a tragedy not only in the Greek sense, but also because the main character Willy Loman qualifies as a truly tragic figure. Willy follows the wrong dream, something that can happen to any one of us. The pain and humiliation, the tragedy and moral loss in any situation like Willy's are hugely painful to witness.

Moral issues make stories work and Terry Malloy in *On the Waterfront* obeys moral authority by choosing to inform on the corrupt union officials. Part of Terry's transformation involves thinking for himself, thereby forging an identity.

In the novel, *East of Eden,* the narrator maintains that the struggle between good and evil is the one recurring narrative of human history. He goes so far as to state that there "is no other story". *East of Eden* makes it very clear, through some remarkable relationship acting, that the lack of parental love or affection can be destructive and dismal. It inspires us to avoid that route in our own relationships. Although one of the fundamental ideas in the film is that evil is an innate and inescapable human problem, the story also sets out hope that each individual has the freedom to choose a path.

Seeing dignity in others can cause great emotional upheaval amongst us in an audience. In the early scenes of *Moby Dick*, dignity is plainly visible on the faces of the men and women. The images of the women suffering as they watch their men go off to sea are utterly devastating; they hold so much emotional depth particularly as we see and hear Orson Welles give his fine performance as Father Mapple.

Grabbing (and keeping) attention is something that clever anti-war films can do but there are very few that do it well. *All Quiet on the Western Front* does it with pathos and a depiction of the violence and sadness inherent in the tearing up of young people's lives; that's a clever stance because we also see it from the German point of view and we are shocked by the shocks faced by the very young German soldiers as they face the front. *Paths of Glory* is perhaps more predictable, but that doesn't lessen our emotion towards the story and we still become very angry at man's stupidity, greed and crass disrespect for life. We snort with derision at French follies in the war here but actually, faced with similar dilemmas, some people have always done the same. The story, while one of loss, is also full of understanding and compassion.

Many people don't seem to reflect much on big issues where mistakes are admitted or direction change is considered. *The Browning Version's* Crocker-Harris certainly does though, despite the realisation coming late, perhaps too late. Crocker-Harris mourns the loss of the classics: "How can we mold civilized beings if we no longer believe in civilization?" The story unfolds a little like a foregone conclusion and we don't empathise with the protagonist until perhaps towards the story's end when the full import of his, the school's and wider society's change hits us firmly in the head and heart.

Chapter Four

THE 1960s

"Sir Thomas More: You threaten like a dockside bully.
Cromwell: How should I threaten?
Sir Thomas More: Like a minister of state. With justice.
Cromwell: Oh, justice is what you're threatened with.
Sir Thomas More: Then I am not threatened."
Sir Thomas More (Paul Schofield) and Cromwell (Leo McKern) in *A Man for all Seasons* (1966)

I was introduced to the Twist and a song by Chubby Checker called *Let's Twist Again* in the 1960s. The Beatles were big and brilliant in the '60s. Pink Floyd began. Marilyn Monroe died in 1962 and that was also the year of the Cuban Missile crisis. President John F. Kennedy was assassinated in 1963. Boxer Cassius Clay changed his name to Muhammad Ali. Miniskirts appeared in 1965. President Johnson ordered bombing raids on North Vietnam in the same year. Christian Barnard undertook the first heart transplant in South Africa in 1967 and Martin Luther King Jr. and Robert Kennedy were both assassinated in 1968. In 1969, the Woodstock music festival took place in upper-state New York. (I was there and it was extraordinarily inspirational.) Also in 1969, a man landed on the moon. Cinema and theatre in the 1960s reflected the decade of fun, revolution, fashion, rock 'n' roll and social change.

The laser was invented in 1960, light emitting diodes (LEDs) in 1962, the computer mouse in 1963, the automated teller machine (ATM) in 1967, the same year Texas Instruments gave us the first hand-held calculator (and check out the cost of one of those!).

Memorable TV shows of the 1960s included *The Monkees, The Saint, The Benny Hill Show, Monty Python's Flying Circus, Peyton Place, The Fugitive, The Man From UNCLE, Mr. Ed* and *I Dream of Jeannie.* Universal began its famed studio tours in 1964 and Disney created a theme park – DisneyWorld in Orlando, Florida. Some studios found it hard to manage financially and a number were acquired by other unrelated businesses. Others tried to tempt audiences by being lavish in production. For example, Joseph L. Mankiewicz directed *Cleopatra* (1963) for 20th Century Fox at a huge cost (then) of $44m. The film paired Elizabeth Taylor and Richard Burton and, while it grossed very big sums for the time, still made a considerable loss. Actually, Fox was saved from financial disaster by the war epic, *The Longest Day* (1963), starring Richard Burton, Sean Connery and Henry Fonda, amongst others. Fox also did well with *The Sound of Music* (1965).

To cut costs, many American studios made their films outside the US, with a fair few looking to the UK where, for example, *Becket* (1964) directed by Peter Glenville was made, with Richard Burton in the titular role and Peter O'Toole as Henry II.

David Lean made his mark as a director of several superb epics during this decade, the first of which was the wonderful *Lawrence of Arabia* (1962) with Peter O'Toole in his first major role. The screenplay was by Robert Bolt who later wrote *A Man for All Seasons* (1966) adapted from his radio and stage plays of the same name. This film won six Academy Awards.

David Lean also gave us the epic *Doctor Zhivago (*1965), adapted from Boris Pasternak's Nobel Prize-winning novel about the days of Russia's Civil War. British cinema came into its own with gritty films depicting the grimness of working-class Britain, social realism and broken relationships. Tony Richardson directed a *Taste of Honey* (1961) and *The Loneliness of the Long Distance Runner* (1962). Clive Donner directed an adaptation of Harold Pinter's *The Caretaker* in 1963. Lindsay Anderson directed *This Sporting Life* (1963) and the intriguing *If* (1969). John Schlesinger directed *A Kind of Loving* (1962) and *Billy Liar* (1963).

The world, and in particular America, also became interested in British fashion, music and culture. *Tom Jones* (1963) was based on the hero of Henry Fielding's classic 18th century novel. The film won four Oscars and director Tony Richardson delivered a funny and bawdy romp that was right for the times. The world took to The Beatles and *A Hard Day's Night* (1964), directed by Richard Lester, depicted a day in the life of the most famous band ever. *Help!* (1965) was also directed by Lester and the story didn't really matter as it was just great to see and hear these four stars being clever and witty all over again. *Yellow Submarine* (1968) showcased the Beatles' work but not the band itself. However, it broke the mould of how animated films could be made.

Other British films such as John Schlesinger's *Darling* (1965) and *Far From the Madding Crowd* (1967) and Lewis Gilbert's *Alfie* (1966) put now famous names on the map: Julie Christie, Lynn Redgrave, Michael Caine, Vanessa Redgrave, Glenda Jackson. The sparkling performance by Maggie Smith in *The Prime of Miss Jean Brodie* (1969) directed by Ronald Neame and based on the novel by Muriel Sparke, still works today. In the 1960s it also became very trendy to watch foreign films. Examples include Federico Fellini's *La Dolce Vita* (1960) and *8 1/2* (1963), Jean-Luc Godard's *A Bout De Souffle* (1960) and the magical Francois Truffaut's *Jules Et Jim* (1962), the latter of which is an absolute must if you've never seen it. From Japan we had Akira Kurosawa's *Yojimbo* (1961) and *Sanjuro* (1962). There was Luchino Visconti's *The Leopard* (1963), Jean-Pierre Melville's *Le Samourai* (1967) and Jacques Tati's brilliant *Playtime* (1967).

Some films, such as *Spartacus* (1960), directed by Stanley Kubrick, became huge over time. Kubrick also made *Lolita* (1962), *Dr. Strangelove: Or, how I Learned to Stop Worrying and Love the Bomb* (1964) and *2001: A Space Odyssey* (1968), based on the novel by Arthur C. Clarke. All three drew mixed reviews. And then there was *Easy Rider* (1969), with its fantastic rock soundtrack, directed by Dennis Hopper, which has a huge following even now.

The Spy Who Came in From the Cold (1965), adapted from the John Le Carré novel, was among the films highlighting the deteriorating relationship between the West and the Soviet Union. The decade also saw the introduction of Ian Fleming's spy, James Bond, to the silver screen, starting with *Dr. No* (1962) directed by Terence Young and the first of six films starring Sean Connery. Literature featured as the source of more films. Leon Uris' *Exodus* (1960) became a film of the same name directed by Otto Preminger. Harold Robbins introduced many a teenager, including me, to the world of vice and sex. His novel, *The Carpetbaggers*, was made into a film in 1964, directed by Edward Dmytryk. Franco Zeffirelli's sexy version of *Romeo and Juliet* (1968) was fresh and still works well.

The Great Escape (1963), directed by John Sturges, stands the test of time as the brilliant movie about escape in World War II. Another film that now has classic status is *Zulu* (1964) directed by Cy Endfield. It put Michael Caine on the map. Other memorable films from the decade include: *The Dirty Dozen* (1967), a tough, all-star never-a-dull-moment film directed by Robert Aldrich, *The Thomas Crown Affair* (1968) by Norman Jewison, *In the Heat of the Night* (1967) also by Jewison, *The Pink Panther* (1964) directed by Blake Edwards and Dustin Hoffman's debut film *The Graduate* (1967), directed by Mike Nichols.

Other classics include the brilliant Clint Eastwood in *A Fistful of Dollars* (1964) directed by Sergio Leone, who also directed *For a Few Dollars More* (1965) and *The Good, The Bad and the Ugly* (1966). These films set a new tone and theme for cowboy movies. Eastwood's films had more in common with John Sturges' *The Magnificent Seven* (1960) with music that most of us can hum even now. They differed from Sam Peckinpah's violent *The Wild Bunch* (1969).

The mesmerising epic of *How the West Was Won* (1963) was directed by Henry Hathaway, John Ford and George Marshall. I went with my father to a huge marquee and watched the three screen Cinerama experiment with joy and wonder. Parts of it still make me weep. And then there was *Butch Cassidy and the Sundance Kid* (1969) directed by George Roy Hill and starring Paul Newman and Robert Redford. The cameraderie and gentle good humour gave the movie huge appeal.

From Walt Disney, there was *Jungle Book* (1967), *101 Dalmatians* (1960), and of course, *Mary Poppins* (1964).

To Kill a Mockingbird (1962) is an adaptation of Harper Lee's novel about a 1930s small-town, widowed southern lawyer (Oscar-winning Gregory Peck as Atticus Finch) who defended a falsely-accused black man against charges of the rape of a white woman. It is compulsive and moving, beautifully written (as is the novel) and cleverly acted. It's probably the most inspirational film I've ever seen.

FROM THE FILM

25 INHERIT THE WIND

DIRECTED BY STANLEY KRAMER (1960)

Jerome Lawrence and Robert Edwin Lee wrote the play from which this film was adapted in 1955. It is a parable that fictionalises the real 1925 Scopes Trial, which resulted in the prosecution of John Scopes, a teacher in Tennessee, who was accused of teaching and condoning Charles Darwin's theory of evolution.

The movie version portrays with poetic licence the famous and dramatic courtroom battle between lawyers Clarence Darrow and William Jennings Bryan. The confrontation between Tracy and March in the witness stand uses dialogue straight from the Scopes trial transcripts. The controversy of evolution versus creationism still rages today, particularly in parts of the US.

THE STORY

A young high school maths and science teacher called Cates (Dick York) is accused of breaking state law by instructing children in Darwin's theory of evolution. Cates (like the original Scopes) wants his day in court so that he can show that creationsism is nonsense.

In both the play and film versions of *Inherit the Wind*, the names and places are changed, but the basic chronology of the real case is retained, along with most of the original court transcripts. In the film version, Bertram Cates represents John Scopes; Henry Drummond (Spencer Tracy) is Clarence Darrow and Matthew Harrison Brady (Fredric March) is William

Jennings Bryan. While Bryan won the case, as most thought he would, with reasonable ease, he and his fundamentalist supporters were held up to ridicule by the stealthy and clever Darrow.

At the end of the trial Cates is found guilty and fined a token $100. Brady is furious at the outcome and the meagre punishment, causing him to have a heart attack during his final speech and dying a little later. The trial's real winner is Drummond, who gains a moral victory, proving his adversary to be something of a fool, and rejects the fine, insisting on an appeal.

Alone in the final scene in the courtroom, Drummond sees a copy of Darwin's *Origin of the Species* and a Bible. He weighs them one in each hand, looking bemused and thoughtful, then shrugs and bangs the two books together.

THE SPEECH

Drummond is considering the Bible's truths and examining prosecuting lawyer Brady. His speech completely sinks the opposition's argument and we feel somewhat vindicated that Brady's argument is dying but we are also inspired because logic and sense are winning the day. Most of us feel we have right on our side and being part of the winning side is in itself inspirational. The language of argument here is also superb. That too is inspirational.

> “You believe that every word written in this book should be taken literally? ... Now what about this part right here, where it talks about Jonah being swallowed by the whale? You figure that really happened? ... Now I recollect a story about Joshua – Joshua making the sun stand still. As an expert, do you tell me that that's as right as the Jonah business? That's a pretty neat trick ... If, in the beginning, there were just Cain and Abel, and Adam and Eve, where did this extra woman come from? ... The Bible is a book. It's a good book. But it is not the only book ...”

In reality, the trial had never been about a teacher's guilt or innocence. It had always only been about exposing a law that made no sense.

FROM THE ANTHOLOGY

26 THE HOLLOW CROWN

This is a collation for the stage of a group of writings and extracts devised by John Barton in 1961. In 1960, along with Peter Hall, Barton co-founded the Royal Shakespeare Company where he has since been a director and advisor for four decades. The anthology presents, in dramatic form, speeches, documents, conversations and music, all linked in some way to the British monarchy – from William the Conqueror to Queen Victoria. It sparkles with the wit of several centuries and demonstrates the vulnerable humanity, incapability or wickedness of real men and women who have played out their lives in getting to or being on England's throne.

The Hollow Crown has been produced for the stage many times and has starred Shakespearean actors and luminaries including the likes of Vanessa Redgrave, Sir Donald Sinden, the late Ian Richardson and an acting hero of mine, Alan Howard.

THE STORY

There isn't one as such, but Shakespeare's *Richard II* explains the collection admirably.

It begins with the premise that Richard believes himself to be of royal blood by divine right and therefore is God's deputy. Richard is gifted and bright, but politically weak. John of Gaunt, the Duke of Lancaster, is Richard's uncle and father of the king's rival, Henry Bolingbroke.

Richard wages war in Ireland, but needs money to support the action. John of Gaunt is rich and, when he dies, Richard confiscates his property. Bolingbroke and many nobles rebel against the king, thinking he'll do the same to them. Richard yields and Henry escorts him to London. The king signs a confession and rescinds the throne. Henry orders him to be confined to the Tower of London, then announces his own coronation as Henry IV. The Duke of Aumerle, the Bishop of Carlisle and the Abbot of Westminster organise a last-minute plot against Henry, but it fails badly. Henry has Richard transferred to Pomfret Castle. When Bolingbroke, as the new king, asks whether anyone will rid him of Richard, Sir Pierce of Exton assumes that Bolingbroke wants him dead. With two assistants, he kills Richard. Henry is full of guilt and, although Exton reminds Henry that he wished Richard dead, Exton is banished.

THE SPEECH

There are several speeches which are inspirational. This one is taken from Act III and actually contains the phrase, "the hollow crown":

"DUKE OF AUMERLE:
Where is the duke my father with his power?

KING RICHARD II:
No matter where; of comfort no man speak:
Let's talk of graves, of worms, and epitaphs;
Make dust our paper and with rainy eyes
Write sorrow on the bosom of the earth,
Let's choose executors and talk of wills:
And yet not so, for what can we bequeath
Save our deposed bodies to the ground?
Our lands, our lives and all are Bolingbroke's,
And nothing can we call our own but death
And that small model of the barren earth
Which serves as paste and cover to our bones.
For God's sake, let us sit upon the ground
And tell sad stories of the death of kings;
How some have been deposed; some slain in war,
Some haunted by the ghosts they have deposed;
Some poison'd by their wives: some sleeping kill'd;
All murder'd: for within the hollow crown
That rounds the mortal temples of a king
Keeps Death his court and there the antic sits,
Scoffing his state and grinning at his pomp,

Allowing him a breath, a little scene,
To monarchize, be fear'd and kill with looks,
Infusing him with self and vain conceit,
As if this flesh which walls about our life,
Were brass impregnable, and humour'd thus
Comes at the last and with a little pin
Bores through his castle wall, and farewell king!
Cover your heads and mock not flesh and blood
With solemn reverence: throw away respect,
Tradition, form and ceremonious duty,
For you have but mistook me all this while:
I live with bread like you, feel want,
Taste grief, need friends: subjected thus,
How can you say to me, I am a king?"

I make no excuse for quoting such a chunk because it's beautiful language. There's inspiration just in that language. Richard is convinced of himself and his right to power; he does not recognise that reality is different from his imagination. This speech is inspirational because it breathes a sadness, a misunderstanding of a king's role perhaps, and a hope that people recognise greatness. The speech makes us want Richard to be strong and great. The fact that he will be neither (in this play) doesn't diminish the inspiration that the speech instills.

FROM THE FILM

27 JUDGMENT AT NUREMBERG

DIRECTED BY STANLEY KRAMER (1961)

This film is based on the real-life trials of a number of Nazis, members of Hitler's administration, between 1948 and 1949. It focuses on the trial of four men, previously judges in Nazi Germany. The core point revolves around the involvement of men responsible for enforcing laws that were obviously unjust and caused a huge number of deaths of innocent people, particularly in the concentration camps. The narrative is based on true events that came to light at the Nuremberg trials. Included in the film is footage of the concentration camps, which makes one tighten the jaw and clench the fist even now, as much as it must have done then.

THE STORY

Judge Hayward (Spencer Tracy) is overseeing an American tribunal. The four German judges in court include Dr. Ernst Janning (Burt Lancaster) and Emil Hahn (Werner Klemperer) – both accused of sentencing innocent men to death on the instructions of, or in collusion with, the Nazi regime. Representing the defence is Hans Rolfe (Maximillian Schell) and prosecuting is Colonel Tas Lawson (Richard Widmark). The age-old issue here is one of responsibility and the defence of "I was only following orders". Compounding this is the fact that the Allies want to forget the past and focus on the future. But there are those who cannot let what has gone before just disappear.

In his cell, Janning tells Judge Hayward that he truly didn't know the outcome of what he did. In a powerful moment, Hayward tells him that, of course, Janning "knew". He tells Janning that the first time Janning signed an order for a man's execution, Janning knew the man was innocent.

The American tribunal finds all four judges guilty and each receives life imprisonment. Hayward maintains that the judgment is as much about the loss of one life as it is of millions. He maintains that the German people are culpable for standing by and doing nothing and haven't come to terms with their guilt as a nation. There is an eagerness around the court to forget and move on. One's feelings at the film's end are raw.

THE SPEECH

Dr Ernst Janning gives the tribunal a confession that turns out to be brave. It is inspirational – a guilty man realising his guilt and coming to terms with a terrible truth and wanting to ensure that others face up to the same truth. Janning confesses not just for himself, but for every German citizen, despite the angry protest of his defence lawyer who tells the court that his client isn't aware of what his words mean. Janning shouts back:

> "... I am aware. I am aware! My counsel would have you believe we were not aware of the concentration camps. Not aware. Where were we? Where were we when Hitler began shrieking his hate in the Reichstag? Where were we when our neighbours were being dragged out in the middle of the night to Dachau? Where were we when every village in Germany has a railroad terminal where cattle cars were filled with children being carried out to their extermination? ... I am going to tell them the truth ... Werner Lammpe, an old man who cries into his Bible now, an old man who profited by the property expropriation of every man he sent to a concentration camp. Friedrich Hofstetter, the "good German" who knew how to take orders, who sent men before him to be sterilised like so many digits. Emil Hahn, the decayed, corrupt bigot, obsessed by the evil within himself. And Ernst Janning, worse than any of them because he knew what they were and he went along with them ..."

The writing is outstanding and the screenplay rightly won an Oscar for Abby Mann. The speech makes us feel, for a moment at least, inspired by a character standing up for truth. It's a start.

FROM THE MUSICAL AND FILM

28 WEST SIDE STORY

(MUSICAL IN 1957, FILM IN 1961)

Like its stage counterpart, the film is an enormously powerful musical based on Shakespeare's *Romeo and Juliet*. The setting is the Upper West Side of New York City in the late 1950s with conflict between rival street gangs, the Jets (working class white teenagers) and Sharks (Puerto Rican teenagers). It is one of the best film adaptations of a musical ever made. The original stage musical (1957) was a hit with music by Leonard Bernstein and Stephen

Sondheim's lyrics. The film, co-directed by Robert Wise and Jerome Robbins and choreographed by Jerome Robbins received ten Academy Awards.

THE STORY

Puerta Rican Maria (Natalie Wood) meets white American Tony (Richard Beymer). They fall in love, but know that their relationship is dangerous and must be kept secret. Maria's brother Bernardo – leader of the Sharks (George Chakiris) – kills Riff (Russ Tamblyn), leader of the Jets and one of Tony's friends. Tony in turn kills Bernardo. The story more or less follows the Shakespearean version and Tony gets killed at the end although Maria doesn't die. Tony's death brings the two gangs together.

THE SPEECH

The level of inspiration throughout is high. There is often hope that is dashed and dashed hope that rises again. At the story's close, the death of a hero gives some closure. It's the essence of tragedy, but in the end here hope is on the rise and doesn't wane; we are invited to believe that some good will come out of bad. At the film's end, Maria shouts at Chino, Bernado's best buddy (played by Jose DeVega) who has just killed Tony:

> “Stay back! ... How do you fire this gun, Chino? By pulling this little trigger? How many bullets are left, Chino? Enough for you? Or you? All of you! You all killed him! And my brother! And Riff! Not with bullets and knives! With hate! Well, I can kill now too, because now I have hate! How many can I kill, Chino? How many – and still have one bullet left for me? Don't touch him!”

The struggle of Maria and Tony to love each other in the face of opposition ends on a hopeful note. The two gangs, confused, stunned and eventually ashamed by the unnecessary killings, finally put aside their enmity. As some of the Jets struggle to carry Tony's body away, a few of the Sharks assist them. We *are* inspired as hope kicks in.

FROM THE FILM

29 TO KILL A MOCKINGBIRD

DIRECTED BY ROBERT MULLIGAN (1962)

This film is an adaptation of the Pulitzer prize-winning novel by Harper Lee published in 1960. Like the book, the film deals with two important topics: individual worth over the colour of someone's skin and justice. Gregory Peck, who played Atticus Finch in the film (and rightly won an Oscar for it), was a civil rights activist and said he liked the role of Atticus more than any other in his career.

THE STORY

The narrator is tough six-year-old Scout (Mary Badham), the daughter of Atticus who is a widowed lawyer with a practice in Maycomb. Scout's narration, beginning with her childhood, takes us on a journey through the injustice and intolerable prejudice of Alabama in the early 1930s. She, her brother Jem (Philip Alford) and their friend Dill (John Megna) all have an idyllic time and are mischievous and happy children. Nothing much ever happens in Maycomb but one day Tom Robinson (Brock Peters), a young black man, is falsely accused of raping a poverty-stricken white woman. Morally stout Atticus is appointed by the court to defend Tom for whom a guilty verdict from an all-white jury is a given. Besides, the town would rather lynch Tom than see him tried and the prevalent bigotry makes life for Atticus and his family difficult.

The trial becomes the mainstay of the story against which everything happens. There is the eccentric Boo Radley (Robert Duvall) whom the children think is insane and he disappears for chunks of time. The kids find small gifts in a tree outside Boo's house – for example a cigar box with a collection of trinkets in it – and they begin to revise their view of the strange man.

During the trial – which Atticus forbids the children to attend but which they see anyway – Atticus tries to show that Mayella (Collin Wilcox), the woman Tom has allegedly raped, and her father, Bob Ewell (James Anderson), have been lying and that the rape charge is cooked up. It becomes clear that Mayella had been making advances to Tom when her father caught them kissing. However, no matter what proof Atticus offers, Tom is found guilty He is shot and killed while attempting to escape from prison.

Ewell feels humiliated by the trial and swears revenge on Atticus. When he attacks Scout and Jem in the street, the mysterious Boo Radley comes to their aid and disappears once he has helped rescue the children. In the fight, Ewell is killed. It's agreed that the story will be that Ewell fell on his own knife and that no blame shall attach to the children.

THE SPEECH

Atticus Finch's closing argument to the jury, imploring them to acquit the innocent Tom, is simply one of the best pieces of film oratory ever. It soars, transfixes and moves. It gives hope and manages to echo the defence's humility and honour, dignified by righteousness. It is inspiration incarnate. If there was an order of favourites in this book, this would be my first:

"... To begin with, this case should never have come to trial. The State has not produced one iota of medical evidence ... It has relied instead upon the testimony of two witnesses whose evidence has not only been called into serious question on cross examination, but has been flatly contradicted by the defendant. Now there is circumstantial evidence to indicate that Mayella Ewell was beaten savagely by someone who led, almost exclusively, with his left. And Tom Robinson now sits before you, having taken the oath with the only good hand he possesses – his right. I have nothing but pity in my heart for the chief witness for the state. She is the victim of cruel poverty and ignorance, but my pity does not extend so far as to her putting a man's life at stake, which she has done in an effort to get rid of her own guilt ... Now what did she do? She tempted a Negro ... She did something that in our society is unspeakable. She kissed a black man ... Now ... I am confident that you gentlemen will review – without passion – the evidence that you have heard, come to a decision, and restore this man to his family. In the name of God, do your duty. In the name of God, believe Tom Robinson.”

Several hours after the verdict and after the court has cleared, as Atticus walks towards the exit at the back of the court, the black people in the balcony stand to show respect as he passes through the courtroom. Even Scout is urged to stand in his honour by the Reverend Sykes:

> “Miss Jean Louise, stand up, your father's passin'.”

Doesn't this line alone show the worth of honour in praise of truth even though it did little good? Was the good done for the future? Or were no lessons learnt?

FROM THE FILM

30 LAWRENCE OF ARABIA

DIRECTED BY DAVID LEAN (1962)

This is a brilliant epic starring Peter O'Toole. Robert Bolt co-wrote the script with Michael Wilson. It is largely about T. E. Lawrence and the British army during World War I in what was then Arabia. The film focuses on Lawrence's attacks on Aqaba and Damascus and thereon his role with the Arab National Council. It explores the identity of this mysterious, eccentric and brave man, the violence of war and his commitment to England and Arabia. The film won seven Academy Awards, including Best Picture and Best Director.

THE STORY

Lawrence (Peter O'Toole) is a British Army lieutenant in Northern Africa. He behaves oddly and has no respect for his superiors, thinking them foolish. As he has an in-depth knowledge of the native Bedouin tribes, he is sent on a fact-finding mission to Prince Feisal of Arabia (Alec Guiness), who is a central figure in the insurrection against the occupying Turks. Lawrence suggests a bold plan to take the Turkish held port of Aqaba, which would involve a march across the waterless Nefud Desert – something most would consider impossible.

Using a combination of diplomacy and bribery, Lawrence unites the rival Arab factions of Feisal and Auda Abu Tayi (Anthony Quinn). After successfully completing his mission, Lawrence becomes an unwitting pawn of the Allies, represented by General Allenby (Jack Hawkins) and diplomat Mr. Dryden (Claude Rains), who keep using Lawrence to secure Arab co-operation against the Imperial Powers. While on a spying mission to Deraa, Lawrence is captured and tortured by a sadistic Turkish Bey (Jose Ferrer). In the heat of the next battle against the Turks, Lawrence, bent on revenge, screams "No prisoners!" and relishes the carnage. His men enter Damascus before Allenby and his forces.

The Arabs set up a council to administer the city, but they are tribesmen and nomads, ill-suited to bureaucracy, so they soon abandon most of Damascus to the British. Lawrence is promoted to colonel and then immediately ordered home. The negotiations are left to Faisal and the British and French diplomats. Lawrence is despondent and feels useless.

THE SPEECH

The sea fortress at Aqaba is attacked and, after conquering the city, Lawrence instructs Sherif Ali bin el Kharish to summon Prince Feisal and the Arab army on boats to Aqaba. His own plans are to go back to Cairo to report the victory, but Ali doubts Lawrence's true Arab loyalty. It's the underplaying of the great plan that is inspirational, the quiet determination to succeed, the focus on what can be achieved:

"Lawrence: I'm going to tell the generals – in Cairo. Yes, cross Sinai. Come on.

Sherif: Sinai?

Lawrence: Yes.

Sherif (gesturing to Lawrence's two outcaste servant boys): With these?

Lawrence: They will be all right with me. Look Ali, if any of your Bedouin arrived in Cairo and said, 'We've taken Aqaba', the generals would laugh.

Sherif: I see. In Cairo, you will put off these funny clothes. You will wear trousers and tell stories of our quaintness and barbarity. And then they will believe you.”

While crossing the Sinai, Daud, one of Lawrence's outcaste servant boys, is lost in a sinkhole – and Lawrence is unable to save him. He is beside himself with grief for the boy about whom he cared. Eventually, he and Ferraj, the other young follower, reach Cairo where, despite objections, Lawrence – still in his Arab outfit – marches into the Officer's Club and at the bar orders a lemonade for the thirsty boy.

Initially he is refused because he's not dressed correctly and because he has brought an Arab into the club. This is inspirational. It's a golden moment when the powers-that-be and the petty, racist rules, are tested by someone who has just experienced hardship, tragedy and loss and we feel for him. Just as he is about to be thrown out, Colonel Brighton appears and asks Lawrence to explain himself. Lawrence announces his military success:

“Lawrence: We've taken Aqaba.

Brighton: Taken Aqaba? Who has?

Lawrence: We have. Our side in this war has. The wogs have. We have ...

Brighton: You mean the Turks have gone?

Lawrence: No, they're still there, but they've no boots. Prisoners, sir. We took them prisoners, the entire garrison. No, that's not true. We killed some, too many really. I'll manage it better next time. There's been a lot of killing, one way or another. Cross my heart and hope to die, it's all perfectly true.

Brighton: It isn't possible.

Lawrence: Yes it is. I did it.”

It's the understatement, the matter of factness, that inspires us and put into juxtaposition achievement against grandstanding.

From the film

31 A HARD DAY'S NIGHT

directed by Richard Lester (1964)

This was a mock documentary about a day and a bit in the life of The Beatles, refreshing in that it did not take itself too seriously. It obviously features the Fab Four and stars Wilfred Brambell as Paul's grandfather, Norman Rossington as the band's pressurised manager and John Junkin as the manager's assistant, Shake. The gags are quick and in keeping with how we want The Beatles to be. The whole is a clever, smart and warming film, with genuine comedy and great fun moments. It also moves at a brisk pace – giving fans a kind of closeness and insight into the conversations and behind-the-scene world of a huge phenomenon. That in itself inspires. The film was commercially successful and was a marker for many pop promos that followed.

THE STORY

The seemingly chaotic plot revolves around the band having to get from Liverpool to take part in a TV show on time in London and Paul McCartney's efforts to keep his grandfather, always referred to as a "clean old man", from getting into trouble. Ringo is always walking off for mini-adventures, but his independence lands him in prison for a short while and he nearly misses the London gig. The relationship between the calm and cool John Lennon, always ready with a clever quip, and the harassed band manager, Norm, is great fun, as is the relationship between Norm and his assistant, Shake, who constantly apologises for being taller than his boss. George Harrison features in a great sequence where he is mistaken for someone auditioning for a part in a trendy TV programme. At regular intervals we get to hear hits such as *I Should Have Known Better*, *All My Loving*, *Can't Buy Me Love*, *And I Love Her* and *She Loves You.*

THE SPEECH

There are a few moments in this film that uplift – and none of them are speeches as such. I don't apologise. Here's why. It's the film's simplicity and freshness that make it work and it inspires by the sheer fact that you're watching the biggest band ever in the whole world. That's how it felt then and that's how it feels now.

The first inspirational moment is in the opening sequence, when the band is mobbed at the station as John, Paul, George and Ringo try to get onto the London train. There's a terrific level of energy and excitement – a surge, an adrenaline rush. We feel the hysteria of the fans and the excitement of the Beatles, intercut with the title song (then a new device for a film's opening). The other moment is that strident, opening chord from George Harrison's 12-string Rickenbacker guitar and the suspense as the note is left hanging for a very long breath before the song takes off.

Another moment is the concert footage as the Beatles sing *She Loves You* in the fourth quarter of the film. This is one of the most sustained and inspirational sequences in the film. They perform with joy and fun. The audience can't hear much because they're screaming. We're part of the moment because we've been with them on the journey to the concert.

FROM THE FILM

32 A MAN FOR ALL SEASONS

DIRECTED BY FRED ZIMMERMAN (1966)

This film is based on Robert Bolt's play of the same title about Sir Thomas More. Paul Scofield, who had played More in the West End stage version, also took the role in the film, which won six Academy Awards, including Best Actor for Scofield, Best Director and Best Picture.

The film's account of the principled More, who sacrifices himself rather than give in to change and the religious immorality of his king, resonated with audiences who felt reassured and inspired by his upholding of values against the dishonesty, chaos and greed around him.

THE STORY

Sir Thomas More was the 16th-century (Catholic) Lord Chancellor of England who refused to sign a letter asking the Pope to annul King Henry VIII's marriage to Catherine of Aragon (his first of six wives). More resigned rather than take an Oath of Supremacy declaring the king the supreme head of the Church of England. More's view was the Pope was the church's head answerable only to God.

Both the play and the film show Sir Thomas as a man of principle, motivated by his devout Roman Catholic faith. His rivals, including the ambitious Thomas Cromwell (Leo McKern), are jealous and that jealousy is made deeper because of Sir Thomas' popularity with the people. King Henry VIII (Robert Shaw) wants to divorce his wife in order to marry Anne Boleyn (Vanessa Redgrave) and sire an heir. To do that, he has to break away from the Catholic Church. Sir Thomas willingly goes to the chopping block rather than sacrifice his ideals.

THE SPEECH

Sir Thomas is invited to speak to the court after being found guilty of high treason. What he says is inspirational in its simplicity and quiet dignity. We may want him to rescind and give way – to save his life – but we applaud his passion and commitment to his truth:

> “Since the Court has determined to condemn me, God knoweth how, I will now discharge my mind concerning the indictment and the King's title. The indictment is grounded in an act of Parliament which is directly repugnant to the law of God, and his Holy Church, the Supreme Government of which no temporal person may by any law presume to take upon him …”

The speech continues and is all the more moving because we know, as does he, that his cause is lost now and that he's destined for the executioner.

FROM THE FILM

33 GUESS WHO'S COMING TO DINNER

DIRECTED BY STANLEY KRAMER (1967)

This film launched to mixed reviews. Some saw it as too soft, not really getting to grips with mixed marriage issues. Others saw it as the reverse – too avant garde. It's actually a film that managed to focus with great precision on issues that were by and large taboo in many parts of the US and indeed elsewhere. Mixed marriages had been illegal in most of America and were still illegal in seventeen southern American states until the year of the film's release.

This was Spencer Tracy's last film and it won two Academy Awards, one for Katharine Hepburn as Best Actress.

THE STORY

Matt Drayton (Spencer Tracy) is a wealthy newspaper publisher in San Francisco. His daughter, Joy (Katharine Houghton), returns home from a holiday in Hawaii with the surprising news that she is engaged. Her fiancé is an African-American, Dr. John Prentice (Sidney Poitier), a specialist in tropical medicine. Privately, Dr. Prentice tells Matt that he will only marry Joy if Matt approves. The publisher only has a few hours to make his decision because Dr. Prentice has to be on a flight to Switzerland that evening. After her momentary shock, Matt's wife, Christina (Katharine Hepburn), readily accepts the idea of the marriage. Matt's best friend, Monsignor Ryan (Cecil Kellaway), also approves wholeheartedly.

Joy invites Dr. Prentice's parents to fly up from Los Angeles and join the Drayton family for dinner. John's parents are unaware that Joy is white. When they meet, John's father is angry. Joy makes up her mind to leave on the plane with John that evening. Everyone divides into groups for conversations about the issue, with the two fathers opposing and the two mothers approving. Mrs. Prentice eventually tells Matt that he is a sad old man who has no recollection of what it felt like to be in love. This hits home with Matt who then makes his mind up on the matter and gathers everyone together. Matt's monologue is extraordinarily moving and uplifting. He concludes that if his daughter and John love each other as much as he loved Christina when *they* married, then all will be well. He gives the couple his blessing and dinner is served.

THE SPEECH

Towards the film's end, Matt's speech leads us to believe that love can conquer superstition, racism and social mores. He speaks about his own love for his wife Christina who sits watching and listening – her eyes filling with seemingly genuine tears. Hepburn was very fond of Tracy and knew that he was ill; indeed he died a few weeks after the film was completed.

> “There is nothing, absolutely nothing, that your son feels for my daughter that I didn't feel for Christina. Old? Yes. Burnt out? Certainly. But I can tell you the memories are still there – clear, intact, indestructible. And they'll be there if I live to be 110. Where John made his mistake I think was attaching so much importance to what her mother and I might think. Because in the final analysis, it doesn't matter a damn what we think – the only thing that matters is what they feel and how much they feel for each other. And if it's half of what we felt ... that's everything.”

The speech tells us what we want to hear, what we *need* to hear – openly, precisely and powerfully. It's a salve, an ointment that soothes the soul. And it's necessary.

AN OVERVIEW OF
CHAPTER FOUR

Although the *Inherit the Wind* trial concerns the battle between creationism and evolutionism, a deeper conflict exists beneath the surface. Drummond points to this more basic issue when he asks his young witness, Howard, whether he believes in Darwin. When the boy responds that he hasn't made up his mind, Drummond insists that the boy's freedom to think – to make up his own mind – is what is actually on trial. There is bravery in truth. Kramer's achievement in *Judgment at Nuremberg* is that everything in the film reminds us that the Nazi machine used every facet of civilisation, no matter how minute, to foster the extermination of enemies, to inculcate it as an ordinary part of life. The Nazis prevailed with the willing acquiescence of the German people and the disregard of the rest of the world. The lessons here are wide and deep; none are really learnt and man's inhumanity to man has continued since, often unabated and often little mentioned. The other horror revealed in this film is the incessant attempts at excusing the perpetration of dreadful crimes.

Taking sides is relatively easy in most stories and frequently the plot insists that we do take sides. In *The Hollow Crown*, there are no sides taken. In the trial of Charles I, for example, which pits the monarch against his prosecutor, it's not clear with whom we should sympathise – with the powers of the throne or the claims of 17th-century populism. The issues raised in this play transcend the question of the monarchy's legitimacy, dealing instead with power and authority. Some plays and films are all about the taking of sides. In transferring the idea of *Romeo and Juliet*, the film *West Side Story* manages to create an ideal understanding of Shakespeare's famous work. The musical is emotive and powerful. We are inspired by the hope and we are moved by the power of love. Cynicism aside, these are strong motifs in art and we follow the story's arguments throughout with both relish and apprehension.

The power of argument is clear as a bell in *To Kill a Mockingbird* and so are the power of goodness, strength of character, a clear knowledge of right and wrong and life's hurts. Atticus Finch, one of the screen's true heroes, fights evil with deeds, advice and moral fibre. He sees the decency in his client and, in a closing argument that must have roused the American civil rights movement, begs the jury to vote for justice. Tom's breakdown on the stand is one of the most realistic, emotionally saddening moments you'll ever see. Because he dared to care about a white girl, he now faces almost certain death if convicted, and perhaps even if not convicted.

Hate and stupidity are also themes that run through *Lawrence of Arabia.* It's an excellent analysis of a man wrestling with himself, with his selfish superiors, with his own demons and with the cruel desert environment. It's a deep look at culture clashes which pitted not only the imperialists against the indigenous populations, but also the mercenary practices of the Arab guerillas against the discipline of the British army. In the end, Lawrence himself does not know which side he is on or to which faction he belongs. It's a big story. Few other films have managed to reach this film's poetic greatness.

The innocence of my generation is showcased in *A Hard Day's Night,* the perfect musical for any audience as the Beatles capture a time that can never be repeated. Forty and some years later the timeless youth of the Beatles still shines out and it's quite a shock to see an older Sir Paul these days. Lessons learned are interesting because the film, its banter and humour set a whole process off in a way that other art developed. *A Man For All Seasons* is a cool look at the maxim that a man cannot serve two masters. Here was an age of faith when Christianity exerted the most powerful of influences on thinking. The volume of emotion communicated through the film is palpable. We feel More's hope, morality and bemusement as richly as he conveys each. It's a rich lesson for anyone managing people or facing difficulties in any environment – only possible because of the excellent model. Admiration is a strong word and never more shown in Hepburn's view of Tracy as a person and an actor in *Guess Who's Coming to Dinner.* We are in a great moment of cinema, of fond tenderness and love between two great stars. In his last monologue of the film where he expresses his love for his wife and endorsement of his daughter's marriage, Tracy's words evoke loyalty. Tracy turns to Hepburn with a long look, and the shot is sustained for a few seconds of deliberate silence. What can we see? Watch it.

Chapter Five

THE 1970s

"P.A. Announcer: Attention. Attention. Friday night's movie will be *The Glory Brigade.* Rock'em sock'em kisses you never got. It's Uncle Sam's combat engineers charging side by side with Greek handbags. Showing the world a new way to fight as they use bulldozers like bazookas, bayonnets like bazook-bullets. Starring Victor Mature. That is all." *M.A.S.H* (1970)

Progressive values, political awareness, revolution, experimentation, exploration, more freedoms for women and thirst for social change continued to bloom in the 1970s. Opposition to nuclear weapons and war grew, as did general advocacy for world peace and hostility towards authority and large conglomerates. The oil crisis of the early '70s created a worldwide economic recession.

Chile's Augusta Pinochet led a military coup in 1973. The UK's Margaret Thatcher took power as leader of the Conservative Party in 1979. Japan suceeded on all fronts to become one of the leading industrial powers. The Middle East was wracked by conflict, in particular the Yom Kippur war of 1973. However, late in the decade, the Egyptian-Israeli Peace Treaty was signed. The US withdrew its troops from Vietnam in 1975, bringing to a close an unpopular and messy war with no real winners. China's Mao Zedong died in 1976. The Soviet Union invaded Afghanistan in 1979, leading to a ten-year occupation. The same year, revolution removed the Shah and the Pahlavi dynasty in Iran and put in place an Islamic Republic.

The 1970s gave us the Post-It Note, Rollerblades, the Sony Walkman, the Jumbo jet, floppy disks, lead-free petrol, digital cameras, liquid crystal displays, e-mail, the barcode, in vitro fertilisation, and the MRI scanner. Many criticised it as being the decade of selfishness.

Some long-running TV shows began: *The Waltons, Starsky and Hutch, The Muppet Show, Charlie's Angels, Little House on the Prarie, Kojak*, and *Happy Days*. Literary output was wide and deep. We had the play *Accidental Death of an Anarchist* by Dario Fo and Peter Shaffer's *Sleuth* in 1970 and an amazing new production of *A Midsummer Night's Dream* directed by Peter Brook in 1979 for the Royal Shakespeare Company. Richard Bach's *Jonathan Livingston Seagull* (1972) was a major seller and Ira Levin delivered *The Stepford Wives*. In 1973 we had Gore Vidal's *Burr* and the hugely entertaining *La Cage aux Folles*, a French farce by Jean Poiret which became a very funny film in 1978 and a reasonably successful musical in 1983. In 1974, Carl Bernstein and Bob Woodward gave the world the shattering *All the President's Men*, the film of the same name following in 1976. From Peter Benchley the novel *Jaws*, which also spawned the film. *Shōgun* by James Clavell was published in 1975, as was *Ragtime* by E.L. Doctorow. Alex Hayley's amazing opus, *Roots: The Saga of an American Family*, came out in 1976. In 1978 we had *Whose Life Is It Anyway?* by Brian Clark, and John Irving's *The World According to Garp*. 1979 saw the delivery of William Styron's terrifying *Sophie's Choice*, Norman Mailer's *The Executioner's Song, A Bend in the River* by V.S Naipaul and, on stage, *Amadeus* by Peter Shaffer, based on the lives of Mozart and Salieri.

War was the theme for two of the period's most successful films: *Patton*, about the World War II general, and *M*A*S*H* (following a superb TV series). *Apocalypse Now* (1979) directed by Francis Ford Coppola and *The Deer Hunter* (1978) directed by Michael Cimino were about the Vietnam war.

Sean Connery returned to the role of Bond in *Diamonds Are Forever* (1971) before Roger Moore succeeded him in 1973 with *Live and Let Die*, followed by *The Man with the Golden Gun* in 1974.

Asian cinema of the 1970s was on the rise. In the Bollywood of India this was epitomised by the movies of Amitabh Bachchan. The early 1970s also saw the popularity of martial arts films featuring Bruce Lee, who starred in three successful movies: *The Big Boss* (1971), *Fist of Fury* (1971) and *Return of the Dragon* (1972). But it was probably *Enter the Dragon* (1973) that made him a global star and many regard this film as *the* classic martial arts movie.

Airport (1970) was a very successful adaptation of Arthur Hayley's novel and it set a pattern for a large number of disaster movies during this decade and beyond. The ingredients were always an amalgam of suspense, intricate plot, wide-ranging sub-plots and an array of famous actors. Examples include *The Poseidon Adventure* (1972) and *The Towering Inferno* (1974).

The Godfather (1972) directed by Francis Ford Coppola was an absolutely brilliant adaptation of the Mario Puzo novel and deservedly won a clutch of Academy Awards. *The Godfather: Part II* followed in 1974. De Niro featured in another classic, *Taxi Driver* (1976). *Network* (1976) took the lid off the world of TV programme-making and featured the wonderful and often undervalued Peter Finch, who won a posthumous Oscar for his role here. *Rocky* (1976) led to four sequels.

Kubrick's *A Clockwork Orange* (1971) focused on a frightening future world. Other horror or disturbing films included *The Exorcist* (1973), *Marathon Man* (1976), *The Omen* (1976), and *Alien* (1979). There was *Jaws* (1975), Steven Spielberg's first big Hollywood outing and Milos Forman's brilliant *One Flew Over the Cuckoo's Nest* (1975). Other great hits included *Star Wars* (1977), *Close Encounters of the Third Kind* (1977) and the first of the *Superman* series in 1978.

On a comedic note, Woody Allen came up with *Annie Hall* in 1977. Musically, *Saturday Night Fever* (1977) became huge as did *Grease* (1978). Peter Seller's last film, *Being There,* (1979) is terrific. There was also a plethora of crime and gritty detective films: *The French Connection* (1971), the excellent Michael Caine vehicle *Get Carter* (1971) and *Shaft* (1971). *Dirty Harry* (1971) was a great success – followed by four more of the Clint Eastwood vehicles within the franchise. Let's start with Mr Eastwood.

FROM THE FILM

34 DIRTY HARRY

DIRECTED BY DON SIEGEL (1971)

This was the first in the *Dirty Harry* series, starring Clint Eastwood as San Francisco Police Department Inspector Harry Callahan.

THE STORY

Callahan is a policeman with no time for rules if they get in the way of catching villains. He achieves results, albeit through unusual means. Now he's tracking down a serial killer, Scorpio (Andy Robinson), who shoots random victims. The killer promises that his next victims will be "a Catholic priest or a nigger" if the city does not pay him $100,000.

Harry and new partner Chico (Reni Santoni) are assigned to hunt Scorpio down, but not before the mayor (John Vernon) and Lt. Bressler (Harry Guardino) admonish Callahan for his heavy-handed tactics. Racing against a deadline to save a kidnap victim from suffocating to death and irritated by the niceties of citizens' rights and search warrants, Callahan brings in Scorpio, only to see him released on technicalities. "The law's crazy", mutters Harry in disgust, before taking it upon himself to ensure that Scorpio doesn't kill again.

THE SPEECH

There's one quote in movie history that's perhaps more memorable than any other. Harry Callahan taunts a wounded criminal on the ground:

"I know what you're thinking. Did he fire six shots or only five? Well, to tell you the truth, in all this excitement, I've kinda lost track myself. But being as this is a .44 Magnum, the most powerful handgun in the world, and would blow your head clean off, you've got to ask yourself one question: 'Do I feel lucky?' Well, do ya punk? (Harry picks up the gun)

Bank robber: "Hey, I gots to know." (Harry pulls the trigger toward the bank robber's head, but it clicks – empty. Harry chuckles.)"

We feel safe with cop Harry around and we like it when he wins against the villains. We like his quips and his snarling disdain for the rules. Few other actors could have played a hero like this whom we like, even though we know he's flawed. Maybe it's because we know he's flawed that we like him. Eastwood's Dirty Harry is a man you really want on your side and that, in a way, is inspiring.

FROM THE FILM

35 FIDDLER ON THE ROOF

DIRECTED BY NORMAN JEWISON (1971)

The film was adapted from the Broadway musical of the same name and won three Academy Awards. It's happy, sad, moving, funny and warm, focusing on a Jewish family in Tsarist Russia when anti-semitism was rife. The songs from the film are memorable and well known – in particular, *If I Were a Rich Man, Tradition* and *Matchmaker Matchmaker.*

THE STORY

Tevye (Topol), the film's narrator, regularly breaks the fourth wall and talks to the camera (us) or has a one-way conversation with God. He is a leader of a small farming community, Anatevka, in early twentieth-century Russia. The village has two parts – one Orthodox Jewish and the other Christian. On the whole, the two communities leave each other alone and get along. Tevye lives on a farm with his long-suffering wife Golde (Norma Crane) and their children, including three daughters each of whom is ready to be married off. Two do so happily with Tevye's permission (vital in those days) although one, Hodel (Michèle Marsh), who marries and then moves away. Chava (Neva Small), the youngest, is not given permission, but breaks tradition and marries someone who isn't Jewish. Eventually, everyone has to leave because the village is about to be destroyed.

This story is well told, and the film beautifully produced and acted. It has hope marred by fear and also fear that is pushed away by hope. Whatever your religion or beliefs, do watch it.

THE SPEECH

The film opens with Tevye telling us, the audience, that being Jewish in Tsarist Russia is a fine balancing act – much like a fiddler on a roof. It is clear that the village might expect a Cossack attack at any time and that life is dangerous and hard. We hear Tevye's introduction as we see a beautiful sunrise; both are uplifting. It's a wonderful start, full of humility, grace and humour:

> “A fiddler on the roof – sounds crazy – but here, in our little village of Anatevka, you might say every one of us is a fiddler on the roof. Trying to scratch out a pleasant, simple tune without breaking his neck. It isn't easy. You may ask, 'Why do we stay up there if it's so dangerous?' Well, we stay because Anatevka is our home. And how do we keep our balance? That I can tell you in one word: tradition! Because of our traditions we've kept our balance for many, many years. Because of our traditions, every one of us knows who he is and what God expects him to do.”

This tale of the emotional turmoil of a family facing upheaval is a powerful and uplifting, inspirational experience. The fact that it's a musical doesn't detract. The reverse is the case – the music, the songs add value.

FROM THE FILM

36 UNDER MILK WOOD

DIRECTED BY ANDREW SINCLAIR (1972)

Originally a radio play completed in 1953 by Dylan Thomas – only months before his death – this beautiful prose-poem-play is a one-off. It is simply brilliant as a piece of radio and equally superb as a piece to read. It also worked well as a film. There were stars galore, including Richard Burton, Elizabeth Taylor and Peter O'Toole.

THE STORY

This delightful narrative of a day in the life of a small, Welsh fishing village called Llareggub (say it backwards) situated under Milk Wood, has no plot, but a wealth of curious characters who dream aloud. We meet the likes of No Good Boyo, Lily Smalls, Polly Garter and Organ Morgan through the "eyes" of Blind Captain Cat. As the village sleeps, a narrator tells us the citizens' darkest hopes, fears and secrets. The feeling is warm and cozy. We are involved, engaged. Dylan Thomas' eye for the absurd and daft captures wonderfully rich, memorable characters.

The language is gentle, lyrical, gossipy, at times energetic and always rich. The true star of the play *is* the language. The words flood our senses and we are part of the celebration of compassion and life.

THE SPEECH

The opening words are magnetic. We immediately get a joyful sense of the goodness of life. We want to read and hear more.

"To begin at the beginning: it is spring, moonless night in the small town, starless and bible-black, the cobblestreets silent and the hunched, courters'-and-rabbits' wood limping invisible down to the sloeblack, slow, black, crowblack, fishingboatbobbing sea. The houses are blind as moles (though moles see fine tonight in the snouting, velvet dingles) or blind as captain Cat there in the muffled middle by the pump and the town clock, the shops in mourning, the Welfare Hall in widows' weeds. And all the people of the lulled and dumbfound town are sleeping now."

FROM THE FILM

37 THE GODFATHER

DIRECTED BY FRANCIS FORD COPPOLA (1972)

This brilliant film, beautifully made, fabulously acted and with terrific writing, is the first of a trilogy. It's also a multi-generational epic about the

Mafia and organised crime in the US, mostly New York. Based on the novel of the same name by Mario Puzo (1969), it won three Academy Awards, including Best Actor for Marlon Brando as Don Corleone.

THE STORY

Michael Corleone (Al Pacino), the family's youngest son, returns from Europe and World War II. Drug dealer Sollozzo (Al Lettieri), who works for the Tattaglia family, asks Don Corleone for his help in selling narcotics. Corleone refuses. Luca Brasi (Lenny Montana), Corleone's bodyguard, is killed when sent to the Tattaglia family to gain some information.

Don Corleone experiences an assassination attempt, but survives. Michael now steps up to the plate and organises the killing of Solozzo and a corrupt police captain named McCluskey (Sterling Hayden), who is in cahoots with the Tattaglia family. Michael shoots them both in a Bronx restaurant after which he flees to Sicily. There, he meets and marries Apollonia, who is later murdered by a car bomb meant for Michael.

One of Michael's two brothers, Sonny (James Caan), who is fiery, wants to deal with brother-in-law Carlo for beating up Sonny's sister Connie. Before he can do so, Sonny is murdered, as a result of which Don Corleone seeks peace with the warring Mafia families. A tougher, harder Michael returns from Sicily and marries his ex-girlfriend Kay (Diane Keaton). The elderly Don Corleone puts Michael in charge of the Family. There are plans to become more legitimate in Las Vegas with the gaming industry. The Family makes an offer to buy out a casino owner, but the offer is refused. Don Corleone dies of a heart attack.

Michael is now the family's head and starts a period of revenge, beginning with the killing of rivals and of Carlo, who had a part in Sonny's death. The movie ends with Michael being the new Godfather, much to the distress of his wife, Kay.

THE SPEECH

The film is, in part, about the evolution and change of Michael Corleone from soft, well-mannered outsider to ruthless, tough and calculating Mafia boss.

The last scene of the film is very powerful indeed. It inspires awe as we witness Michael's sheer power and threat portrayed with utter simplicity. We necessarily like the new Michael because he avenges the Family and we admire his fortitude and strength. Michael refuses to admit responsibility for Carlo's death to either Connie or Kay. Here's his reply when Kay asks about his business:

> "Michael: Don't ask me about my business, Kay.
>
> Kay: Is it true?
>
> Michael: Don't ask me about my business ...
>
> Kay: No.
>
> Michael (slamming his hand on the desk): Enough. All right. This one time, this one time I'll let you ask me about my affairs.
>
> Kay (whispering): Is it true? Is it?
>
> Michael (quietly, shaking his head): No.
>
> Kay (relieved and Michael kisses and hugs her): I guess we both need a drink, huh?"

Kay leaves his study to get a drink, shaky but smiling. Some heavies come in to Michael's study and Kay sees one of the henchmen embracing Michael, obviously acknowledging him as the new Don. The other henchman kisses Michael's ring hand. The power is both inspirational and frightening. Symbolically, the door in Michael's office is shut in Kay's face.

FROM THE FILM

38 ONE FLEW OVER THE CUCKOO'S NEST

DIRECTED BY MILOŠ FORMAN (1975)

This is a classic and enormously successful film, adapted from Ken Kesey's 1962 novel of the same name. The film won five Academy Awards, including Best Actor for Jack Nicholson, Best Director for Forman and Best Actress for Louise Fletcher.

The mental asylum is filled with "cuckoo" patients and the giant, deaf-mute Indian Chief is the one that flies over (and out of) the nest. The novel was originally adapted as a Broadway play starring Kirk Douglas in 1963. Douglas bought the movie rights and his son, Michael, later co-produced the film.

THE STORY

McMurphy (Jack Nicholson) has a string of assault convictions to his name, including a serious charge of underage rape. He convinces the authorities that he's crazy and needs help, rather than prison. In the asylum, he becomes a leading light and helps the other patients gain confidence and have fun. Icy Nurse Ratched (Louise Fletcher) loathes the disruption to her and the hospital's routine and dislikes McMurphy because of his charisma and popularity. He is the cuckoo in the nest.

Once that's clear, we more or less know that McMurphy can't win. But he continues to act in what he considers a fair way, getting the inmates to have a modicum of enjoyment, but eventually goes too far -- with a tragic outcome, the death of young Billy (Brad Dourif). McMurphy blames Nurse Ratched, who has power on her side. She eventually ensures that McMurphy has a lobotomy. Chief Bromden (Will Sampson), about to fly the nest, smothers McMurphy rather than let him live on in such a state.

THE SPEECH

There are many moments when you want to shout out "yippee" because those moments are indeed inspirational and have a power-driven result. Most of the inmates of the hospital have light, comedic qualities, but Indian Chief Bromden isn't one of them. However, towards the film's end, we are inspired by this uncomfortable and large man who has become at ease with himself through McMurphy's influence. Initially unknown to Chief Bromden, McMurphy's had the lobotomy. A catatonic and quiet McMurphy returns to the ward. The spark, the light has gone out:

"Chief Bromden: Mac ... they said you escaped. I knew you wouldn't leave without me. I was waiting for you. Now we can make it, Mac; I feel big as a damn mountain. (He sees the lobotomy scars.)

Chief Bromden: Oh, no ...

Chief Bromden: [Hugging McMurphy] I'm not goin' without you, Mac. I wouldn't leave you this way (Pause) You're coming with me.

Chief Bromden: (Gently letting McMurphy lie down) Let's go. ”

The Chief understands that McMurphy won't be able to escape to Canada as planned. He smothers McMurphy with a pillow. Then, with his tremendous strength and inspired by McMurphy's liberating example, he smashes a window with a heavy marble washstand and escapes from the cuckoo's nest.

FROM THE FILM

39 NETWORK

DIRECTED BY SIDNEY LUMET (1976)

The film is Lumet's brilliant critique of vapid TV journalism where ratings and the story are seen as much more important than any human values. Peter Finch posthumously won a richly deserved Academy Award for Best Actor.

THE STORY

Diana Christensen (Faye Dunaway) is a tough, unprincipled, emotionless, ratings-obsessed TV producer who, at the risk of all else, chases success. Max Schumacher (William Holden) is the married executive who falls for her. Howard Beale (Peter Finch) is an experienced, but ageing network anchorman who's been heartlessly fired because of low ratings. He responds by announcing that he'll kill himself on live television two weeks hence. The station's ratings skyrocket and he becomes a major TV icon with his own show even as he descends into insanity.

Through it all, Beale urges each viewer to repeat the now famous mantra: "I'm as mad as hell, and I'm not gonna take it anymore!" to reclaim our humanity from the medium of rubbish TV. His programme is a huge success, but Beale uses his power to make startling revelations about the station's owners and is assassinated at the film's end by revolutionaries.

THE SPEECH

We watch Beale publicly falling to bits on TV but with what we've seen on television since *Network* came out, it's perhaps not so shocking anymore. Still, Beale's "mad as hell" speech to his viewers is powerful and inspiring. It's a call to arms, a call for help and anger personified.

> "I don't have to tell you things are bad … It's a depression. Everybody's out of work or scared of losing their job … shopkeepers keep a gun under the counter … and there's nobody anywhere who seems to know what to do … we sit watching our TVs while some local newscaster tells us that today we had fifteen homicides and sixty-three violent crimes … and all we say is: 'Please, at least leave us alone ... Let me have my toaster and my TV … and I won't say anything. Just leave us alone.' Well, I'm not gonna leave you alone. I want you to get mad! …. You've got to say: 'I'm a human being … I want all of you to get up out of your chairs. I want you to get up right now and go to the window. Open it, and stick your head out, and yell: 'I'm as mad as hell, and I'm not going to take this anymore!"

FROM THE FILM

40 TAXI DRIVER

DIRECTED BY MARTIN SCORSESE (1976)

This gritty, disturbing, nightmarish film explores issues of alienation in New York, but it could be an urban environment anywhere. The film still has a huge following.

THE STORY

Vietnam veteran Travis Bickle (Robert de Niro) is a loner who hates more or less everyone and everything, particularly the thugs, druggies and parasites who inhabit New York night life. Because he can't sleep, he visits porn movie houses and then drives a yellow cab on a night shift. He tries to get a relationship going with a New York senator's campaign worker, Betsy (Cybil Shepherd), but that's short-lived when he takes her to a porn movie on their first date. He also fails to persuade child prostitute Iris (Jodie Foster) to leave her pimp (Harvey Keitel) and go home to her family. He feels totally inept and buys some handguns with the aim of assassinating the local senator (Leonard Harris), but ends up killing Iris's pimp and a bouncer. Severely wounded himself, he tries to take his own life and fails. We see a recuperated Bickle still driving a cab, but now he's a hero.

THE SPEECH

Bickle's much imitated "You talkin' to me? " scene is delivered (to the camera and an invisible enemy) like a rehearsal for how he'll really behave on the streets. He practices quick-drawing his guns in front of a mirror in his dirty and squalid apartment, saying:

"You talkin' to me? You talkin' to me? You talkin' to me? Then who the hell else are you talkin' to? You talkin' to me? Well, I'm the only one here. Who do the fuck do you think you're talking to?"

The speech and sequence are compelling, edgy and exciting to watch. It's powerful and strangely inspirational, because we want a hero to do something about the streets' lowlifes. We want him to be a knight in slightly dented and dulled armour.

FROM THE FILM

41 ALL THE PRESIDENT'S MEN

DIRECTED BY ALAN J. PAKULA (1976)

This film is based on the book of the same name by Bob Woodward (played by Robert Redford in the film) and Carl Bernstein (Dustin Hoffman), two journalists who investigated Watergate for the *Washington Post* and opened up the ensuing scandal. The film won a couple of Academy Awards and has always been thought of highly for its non-emotional approach to something that rocked America.

THE STORY

This is the true account of the investigation into the Watergate break-in that eventually led to the resignation of President Richard Nixon and covers the period from the June 1972 burglary of the Watergate building (Democratic Party National headquarters) to Nixon's re-election in November later that year. It shows that the burglary was only a very small part of a huge intelligence gathering process that was largely illegal. It also focuses on the tough time the two journalists had in their quest for information.

THE SPEECH

The investigation is fraught with blockages and barriers, including many from the *Washington Post* and the journalists' bosses. *Washington Post* editor Ben Bradlee (Jason Robards) talks to Woodward and Bernstein about their preliminary findings. We know that the speech could go either way – halting the whole process or giving them a green light. We want and get the latter. We want an inspirational view of what small people can do to break the perpetrators of high level wrongdoing:

> “You know the results of the latest Gallup Poll? Half the country never even heard of the word Watergate. Nobody gives a shit. You guys are probably pretty tired, right? Well, you should be. Go on home, get a nice hot bath. Rest up – fifteen minutes. Then get your asses back in gear. We're under a lot of pressure, you know and you put us there. Nothing's riding on this except the, uh, First amendment to the Constitution, freedom of the press, and maybe the future of the country. Not that any of that matters, but if you guys fuck up again, I'm going to get mad. Goodnight.”

From the film

42 MACARTHUR

directed by Joseph Sargent (1977)

This film is inspirational not only because it offers the story of a great American soldier, but also because of the language and beautifully crafted script. Gregory Peck as MacArthur delivers a brilliant performance.

Some say this biopic didn't do justice to MacArthur's reputation, others that his real persona was less than his reputation. This may matter historically, but it doesn't in the context of an inspiring picture of a man who cared about soldiering and the necessity for it.

THE STORY

The film's very beginning gives us MacArthur's extraordinary and final West Point speech which is one of the best examples of oratory ever. From this we find ourselves in the Philippines of 1942, with the Japanese overrunning the country. President Roosevelt (Dan O'Herlihy) instructs MacArthur to leave for Australia and MacArthur bids farewell to his adoring troops. In Australia, he plans to return to the Philippines and force the Japanese out. He accepts the Japanese surrender in 1945.

After World War II, MacArthur leads the process of helping to make Japan a democracy and tries to keep the Russian Communists from overtaking the Orient as they had Eastern Europe. MacArthur is eventually fired from his post by President Truman (Ed Flanders) after the general defies orders during the Korean conflict.

THE SPEECH

For power, rhetoric and soaring uplift, the West Point speech made to cadets in 1962 is simply brilliant. Here's a taste of what tends to be known as the "Duty, Honour, Country" speech:

"Duty, Honor, Country. Those three hallowed words reverently dictate what you ought to be, what you can be, and what you will be. They are your rallying points. They give you a temper of the will, a quality of the imagination, a vigour of the emotions, a freshness of the deep springs of life, a temperamental predominance of courage over timidity, an appetite for adventure over love of ease. In this way, they will teach you to be an officer and a gentleman … From your ranks come the great captains who will hold the nation's destiny in their hands … the soldier, above all other people, prays for peace, for he must suffer and bear the deepest wounds and scars of war ... The shadows are lengthening for me. The twilight is here. My days of old have vanished in tone and tint. They have gone glimmering through the dreams of things that were. Their memory is one of wondrous beauty, watered by tears, and coaxed and caressed by the smiles of yesterday. I listen vainly, but with thirsty ear, for the witching melody of faint bugles blowing reveille, of far drums beating the long roll. In my dreams I hear the crash of guns, the rattle of musketry, the strange, mournful mutter of the battlefield. But, in the evening of my memory, always I return to West Point. Always there echoes and re-echoes: 'Duty, Honour, Country'. ”

In the film, when MacArthur says "I bid you farewell" at the speech's end, there is a beat – but a breath – and then the whole auditorium of cadets rise as one and applaud.

FROM THE PLAY

43 WHOSE LIFE IS IT ANYWAY?

WRITTEN BY BRIAN CLARK (1977)

This play was adapted from Brian Clark's 1972 TV play of the same name. It premiered in London in 1978 starring Tom Conti, and was made into a film in 1981, directed by John Badham and starring Richard Dreyfuss. The film is OK, but the play is brilliant.

THE STORY

On a hospital lies sculptor Ken Harrison who has been paralysed from the neck down in a car accident. He can't sculpt, can't do anything and wants to be allowed to die. Through dialogue and argument between the medical and legal professions and Ken's interventions, we receive two views – one favouring euthanasia and one not. We are left believing that Ken will get his way but, while it is a victory for him, it isn't an emotional victory for us in the audience.

THE SPEECH

There are two moments that I cherish here and neither is a speech, but a moment enhanced by one line. Each line speaks volumes and is inspirational. We are beginning to form our own opinions when a bald statement from Ken shocks:

> “I've decided not to stay alive.”

This is short, inspirational and very powerful. We warm to his decision-making process, his determination and his will, even though we are also aghast at what he means.

At the end of the play we are told that Ken will be allowed to die:

> “I'm afraid you'll have to release your patient.”

This moment is dramatic and powerful; Ken is relieved that he will no longer have to suffer. The audience knows that Ken will now die and that provokes a huge mixture of emotion. We have become attached and don't want to let him go, but we also understand that it is indeed his life anyway.

FROM THE FILM

44 KRAMER VERSUS KRAMER

WRITTEN AND DIRECTED BY ROBERT BENTON (1979)

This film, based on the 1977 novel of the same name by Avery Corman, shows the impact of divorce on a couple and their young son. It received an Oscar for Best Picture.

THE STORY

Ted Kramer (Dustin Hoffman) works in advertising and his work comes before his family. His wife Joanna (Meryl Streep) can't accept this and leaves him so Ted has to take care of housekeeping, himself and young son Billy (Justin Henry). When he has learnt to adjust to his new life, Joanna decides she wants Billy back. The two go to court to fight for the custody of Billy. The court awards custody to Joanna.

On the morning that Billy is to leave his dad, they hug. Joanna calls from downstairs in the lobby and tells Ted that, while she loves Billy and wants him with her, she knows he is already at home and she can't break that up. The ending is optimistic.

THE SPEECH

There are several uplifting and moving moments in the film. One in particular is inspiring. It's the speech where Ted defends his right to have custody of his son. Our sympathies tend to be with Ted because we've observed him change.

"If I understand it correctly, what means the most here is what's best for our son … what law is it that says that a woman is a better parent simply by virtue of her sex? I've had a lot of time to think about what it is it that makes somebody a good parent … it has to do with constancy, it has to do with patience, it has to do with listening to him … It has to do with love … I'm not a perfect parent. Sometimes I don't have enough patience 'cause I forget that he's a little kid. But I'm there … we built a life together and we love each other …"

FROM THE FILM

45 ROCKY II

DIRECTED BY SYLVESTER STALONE (1979)

This was the first sequel in the series. The main members of the original cast all reprised their roles. It was also the first of three Rocky films that Sylvester Stallone not only wrote and starred in, but also directed.

THE STORY

Rocky Balboa (Sylvester Stallone), an unknown boxer, is given a shot at the heavyweight champion, Apollo Creed. Although he fails to win, he does very well and only loses by a split decision. After the fight, Rocky achieves some fame and fortune, marries his fiancée, Adrian (Talia Shire), buys her a fur coat and himself a sports car and a big house.

Rocky tries his hand at commercials, but he can't remember lines and so is forced to work with his brother Paulie (Bert Young) at a meat packing company. He loses his job. Adrian is pregnant and works in a pet shop. Downhearted, Rocky works for his former trainer Mickey (Burgess Meredith) at a gym.

Meanwhile, Apollo wants another match with Rocky to show the world that he can beat the amateur boxer properly. Doctors tell Rocky that another fight might permanently damage an already weakened eye. Adrian doesn't want her husband to fight, but Rocky goes ahead with training. Adrian gives birth to a boy, Rocky Balboa Jr., but goes into a coma. Rocky stops training, but when Adrian recovers, they both agree that the fight should go ahead. Rocky wins and becomes heavyweight champ. It's a typical story of tough becomes good becomes bad becomes good. Funnily enough, it works.

THE SPEECH

Of the many teary moments in the film, one speech in particular can get viewers to clench their fists and say "yes!". It's given by Rocky's normally irritable manager Mickey, who's urging the disheartened Rocky to prepare for his rematch against Apollo:

"Well, Rocky, you got another shot. It's a second shot at the … I don't know, the biggest title in the world. And you're gonna be swapping punches with the most dangerous fighter in the world … But don't lay down in front of him like this! … 'Cause he's gonna kick your face in pieces, you know that? … He wants to bury you … Well, now, I don't, I don't wanna get mad, in a biblical place like this, but I think you're a hell of a lot more than that, kid. A hell of a lot! No, wait a minute. If you wanna blow it … dammit, I'm gonna blow it with you. If you want to stay here, I'll stay with you … Yeah. I'll stay and pray. What I got to lose?"

We know, of course, that Rocky will rise to the bait and go on to win. We're inspired by this David beating his demons and his Goliath.

FROM THE FILM

46 BEING THERE

DIRECTED BY HAL ASHBY (1979)

This was Peter Sellers' last film to be released before his death. It's warm rather than funny, but it's also full of pathos – gentle and inspirational in many ways.

THE STORY

In Washington DC, a middle-aged, simple man called Chance (Peter Sellers) has been an odd-job man and gardener for a wealthy gentleman who has just died. Chance has no idea about the outside world, having been kept indoors by his benefactor for his whole life. Much of Chance's time is spent gardening and watching TV.

After being evicted from the house, Chance is walking the streets of Washington when he's accidentally injured by a car with passenger Eve Rand (Shirley Maclaine), wife of banker and political mentor Benjamin Rand (Melvyn Douglas).

The family insists that Chance recuperates in the Rand family mansion.

When asked his name, Chance says he is Chance the gardener, but he's misunderstood and from that point on is called Chauncey Gardiner. Just about everything he says – which revolves around gardening – is believed to be outstandingly clever and metaphorical. Benjamin Rand invites him to join a meeting with the US president (Jack Warden). Again Chance impresses by his gardening metaphors. He is invited to speak to the press and appears on TV. The authorities try in vain to find something about him but there are no records on the man. Meanwhile, Eve Rand has fallen for Chance.

Benjamin Rand, who has an incurable illness, makes Chance his heir apparent and possible presidental candidate. Chance is also asked to take care of Eve. In the final scene at Rand's funeral, Chance turns and walks across a lake, walking on water. Corny, yes, but the whole thing brings a generous feeling of goodwill.

THE SPEECH

In this case there's a dialogue that, in its simplicity, lifts:

"The president: Mr. Gardner, do you agree with Ben, or do you think that we can stimulate growth through temporary incentives? [long pause]

Chance: As long as the roots are not severed, all is well. And all will be well in the garden.

The president: In the garden.

Chance: Yes. In the garden, growth has it seasons. First comes spring and summer, but then we have fall and winter. And then we get spring and summer again.

The president: Spring and summer.

Chance: Yes.

The president: Then fall and winter.

Chance: Yes.

Rand: I think what our insightful young friend is saying is that we welcome the inevitable seasons of nature, but we're upset by the seasons of our economy.

Chance: Yes! There will be growth in the spring!

Rand: Hmm!

Chance: Hmm!

The president: Hm. Well, Mr. Gardner, I must admit that is one of the most refreshing and optimistic statements I've heard in a very, very long time. [Benjamin Rand applauds]

The president: I admire your good, solid sense. That's precisely what we lack on Capitol Hill.”

We love it because of the simplicity and because we know that naivety is rarely tolerated or accepted as any norm. We are inspired because gentle humility and genuine warmth can count for a lot in a cynical world.

FROM THE FILM

47 AMADEUS

DIRECTED BY MILOŠ FORMAN (1979)

This play written by Peter Shaffer was made into a film in 1984. It won eight Academy Awards. It's a loose picture of Wolfgang Amadeuss Mozart's relationship with his mentor, Antonio Salieri. The play was first performed in London in 1979 and then on Broadway in 1980.

THE STORY

We learn Mozart's story from the perspective of court composer Antonio Salieri, who is presented as a mentor, jealous of Mozart's genius. Salieri speaks directly to the audience many times during the play, his soliloquies serving to move the timeline back and forth. At the beginning, an elderly Salieri speaks to us about his belief that he killed Mozart with poison and then explains his reasons for his hate. And love.

Salieri was initially impressed by Mozart's compositions, but his excitement turned to disappointment when he discovered that Mozart's rough and tumble behaviour did not match the grace and dignity of his beautiful music. Salieri is also upset that God would give the gift of composing beautiful music to someone who has lived a life opposing the Catholic faith. He renounces God and begins to destroy Mozart while pretending to be his friend.

After Mozart's death, Salieri attempts suicide and leaves a note saying he poisoned Mozart, but he survives and, anyway, nobody believes his note.

THE SPEECH

We get that rare insight into how Mozart might have viewed himself. It is this, in the context of what we see in his behaviour and in Salieri's, that is both sad and uplifting. And we not only realise how inspirational Mozart's music is, but also how inspirational Mozart might himself have been:

> "While my father prayed earnestly to God to protect commerce, I would offer up secretly the proudest prayer a boy could think of: Lord, make me a great composer. Let me celebrate Your glory through music and be celebrated myself. Make me famous through the world, dear God. Make me immortal. After I die, let people speak my name forever with love for what I wrote. In return, I will give You my chastity, my industry, my deepest humility, every hour of my life, Amen."

In our mind's eye we can see Mozart, consumed by music, playing, and in our mind's ear, we hear the music. We become intoxicated and inspired, share the thrill and skill that Salieri, consumed by jealousy and ambition, could never match.

FROM THE FILM

48 AND JUSTICE FOR ALL

DIRECTED BY NORMAN JEWISON (1979)

This film, starring Al Pacino, is a courtroom drama and satire against the American justice system. "And justice for all" are the last four words of the American Pledge of Allegiance. Some might argue that the film doesn't stand the test of time, but the acting is excellent and the script is sharp and touching.

THE STORY

Defence lawyer Arthur Kirkland (Al Pacino), who's based in Baltimore, is having a tough time. He has two innocent clients who are languishing in jail and desperate. One dies by suicide and the other is shot by the police. Both deaths were avoidable. Arthur's partner is having an affair and his favourite judge has severe psychological problems. To top it all, another judge – an abhorrent and amoral one – wants Arthur to defend him against a charge of assault. Arthur would like nothing more than to expose the law's corruption, but can he?

THE SPEECH

When Arthur eventually turns on his own client and tells the court that he believes his client, the judge, to be guilty of abusing the young woman he is charged with assaulting, the court's judge tells Arthur he's "out of order" and Arthur famously retorts:

> "*You're* out or order! *You're* out of order! The whole trial is *out of order*!"

It is an inspirational moment and one to be relished. The film finishes with Arthur outside the court knowing that his career and future are probably finished. We're not sure.

AN OVERVIEW OF
CHAPTER FIVE

While the protagonist in *Dirty Harry* isn't necessarily an angel, we admire his rough and tough stance and see in him the brave, tough, no-nonsense hero – very fairy tale in spirit and a very necessary ingredient in storytelling.

It's a strong message and it's clear – good can overcome bad and, in some stories, we need or want to know that from the outset. *Fiddler on the Roof*, while being intelligent and warm, has a serious and menacing undertone of what was happening in Tsarist Russia. The story also underlines the fact that change is a constant threat to some – and a great boon to others.

There is pure joy in listening to beautiful language beautifully delivered. There is a humility in words that can reflect or support our own inner feelings that we sometimes find hard to express. *Under Milk Wood* was conceived for the voice and is one of the best examples of beautiful language telling a simple but everlasting story.

Some plays and films show transformation in a different way and that is no less a lesson in understanding how people change with circumstances and power. In *The Godfather*, the central character undergoes a transformation, resulting in him being almost unrecognisable by the end of the film.

Transformation also features *One Flew Over the Cuckoo's Nest*. The famous final shot ironically happens to be an exit of a major character into that bleak Oregon morning. We all sometimes wish we had a McMurphy-like character next to us to fight for our freedom of choice. The mental hospital in which McMurphy is incarcerated and eventually defeated is a dictatorship in microcosm. The film could be said to be about resurrection and that in itself is inspirational.

There is huge satisfaction to be had in parts of *MacArthur* and, politics or historical verisimilitude aside, the piece that I yearn to hear as frequently as possible is the "Duty, Honour, Country" speech made at West Point on 12 May 1962. If nothing else, we learn how passion and grace, humility and positioning in history can create clarity, purpose and total engagement. Just listen to the real thing and watch the film too.

Being There deals with a simple premise – if you act in a certain way, people will make unquestioned assumptions about you. It's a story of innocence and again, in true storytelling tradition, we like innocence, particularly where, with design or luck, that innocence is protected. Chauncey Gardener, the protagonist in this film, endures a sequence of trials he doesn't understand, saying things that are both omnipresent and absurd. His axioms are no more valuable than when politicians give us an answer which has little gravitas but seems heavy in portent. It is us who add the meaning that wasn't there.

Peril is one of the reasons we watch the performing arts. It's exciting, and for us, safe. In *Amadeus* we can see Mozart's peril even if he can't. On the one hand we hear the great *C Minor Mass, the Requiem* and *Don Giovanni.* On the other we witness a figure for whom we have little sympathy. Mozart's life had the air of tragedy and his undoubted genius speaks to us now. Still. That in itself, like Shakespeare's dramaturgy, is mind-boggling and inspiring.

Chapter Six

THE 1980s

> "An eye for an eye only ends up making the whole world blind."
> From the film *Gandhi* (1982), spoken by Mohandas Gandhi (Ben Kingsley)

The 1980s was a decade of conservative politics marked particularly by Margaret Thatcher in the UK and Ronald Reagan in the US. Argentina invaded the Falkland Islands and the subsequent war with the UK, although short, created tensions in the world, but boosted British morale and standing. There were wars between Iran and Iraq from 1980 to 1988, the Soviet Union and Afghanistan from 1979 to 1989, Lebanon and Israel in 1982. Civil wars broke out in El Salvador from 1980 to 1992, in Sudan in 1983 and Lebanon between 1975 and 1990. China continued to enjoy massive growth, but in 1989 there were student unrests culminating in some being killed by the military in Tiananmen Square.

Microsoft and Apple led the way in the development of (reasonably) cheap computers and software. The IBM PC was launched in 1981 and the Internet was invented by Tim Berners-Lee. Video games became a feature of public entertainment, the mobile phone was a new technology (1988) that grew exponentially. Soft bifocal contact lens were invented in 1983, the disposable camera in 1986, the RU-486 abortion pill in 1988 and Prozac, also in 1988.

Television was used in the UK by Bob Geldoff to explain Ethiopa's tragic famine; the Live Aid concert not only focused on the issue, but raised huge sums and brought together bands that most of us hadn't seen for ages or at all.

John Lennon was assassinated in 1980. In 1981 there were assassination attempts on the Pope and Ronald Reagan. Egyptian President Anwar Sadat was assassinated in 1981 and Prime Minister of India Indira Gandhi in 1984. Prince Charles and Lady Diana Spencer married in 1986. AIDS was identified as a spreading killer disease. Reagan announced a space defence plan called Star Wars. Russia shot down a Korean Airliner. Beirut's US Embassy was suicide-bombed by Hezbollah. In 1984 there was a vast poison gas leak in Bhopal, India, the effects of which are still evident today. In 1985 a hole in the ozone layer was found. The Challenger Space Shuttle exploded in 1986 and in the same year, the Chernobyl nuclear reactor also exploded, with terrible long-term results. The USSR launched the Mir space station. The United States locked horns with Libya, which in turn bombed a German discotheque, killing American soldiers. In 1987 DNA was first used to convict criminals. In 1988, a Pan Am flight was blown up over Lockerbie, Scotland. The Berlin Wall fell in 1989.

Dallas and *Dynasty* were great TV hits, offering glitz, ambition and money galore – ingredients celebrated in films such as *Wall Street (*1987). Long running TV series included *The A-Team, Miami Vice, The Cosby Show* and *Cheers*. In the UK, the BBC introduced *Eastenders* in 1985 (and it's still running). MTV was created and *The Simpsons* first appeared in 1989.

However not all was well everywhere. Many, including the wealthy West, struggled with poverty. Developing countries faced economic and social difficulties and applied for financial assistance from the International Monetary Fund and The World Bank.

In literature, John le Carré's *Smiley's People* came out in 1980; Salman Rushdie brought out *Midnight's Children* in 1981 and Alice Walker's *The Color Purple* was published in 1982. *The Unbearable Lightness of Being* by Milan Kundera followed in 1984 and Robert Ludlum's *The Bourne Supremacy* in 1986. We had *Satanic Verses* by Salman Rushdie in 1988 and Kazuo Ishiguro's *Remains of the Day* in the same year and Amy Tan's *The Joy Luck Club* in 1989.

In the world of theatre there was the different *Children of a Lesser God* (1980) by Mark Medoff, the inspirational *Educating Rita* (1980) by Willy Russell and *The Life and Adventures of Nicholas Nickleby,* first produced in 1980 by the UK's Royal Shakespeare Company based on the Dickens story, and adapted by David Edgar. It was extraordinary. In 1982 we had the very British comedy *Noises Off* by Michael Frayn, and the very American *Glengarry Glen Ross* by David Mamet. 1983 brought us actor and writer Sam Shepherd's great *Fool For Love*. The same year saw *Kiss of the Spider Woman* (*El Beso de la Mujer Araña*) by Manuel Puig, adapted from his novel of the same name. *The Piano Lesson,* a clever Pulitzer Prize winning play by August Wilson, premiered in 1987.

Mammoth films included: Steven Spielberg's and George Lucas' *The Empire Strikes Back* (1980), *Raiders of the Lost Ark* (1981), *E.T: The Extra-Terrestrial* (1982) and *Star Wars: Return of the Jedi* (1983). Among successful films from other directors were *Ghostbusters* (1984), *Romancing the Stone* (1984) and *Back to the Future* (1985) and its numerous sequels. James Bond sequels this decade included: *For Your Eyes Only* (1981) *Octopussy* (1983), *Never Say Never Again* (1983) with a Sean Connery reprise, *A View to a Kill* (1985), *The Living Daylights* (1987) and *Licence to Kill* (1989).

Action and adventure films were *de rigeur* from the likes of Ted Kotchef's *Rambo: First Blood* (1982) and its sequels, to *Aliens* (1986) directed by James Cameron, as a follow-on from *Alien* (1979) directed by Ridley Scott. Spielberg completed his Raiders trilogy with *Indiana Jones and the Temple of Doom* (1984) and *Indiana Jones and the Last Crusade* (1989). Arnold Schwarzenegger leapt to action-fuelled fame in James Cameron's *The Terminator* (1984). Clint Eastwood directed and starred in *Pale Rider* (1985) and Bruce Willis charged in with *Die Hard* (1988) directed by John McTiernan. Tim Burton's visual treat, *Batman (*1989), began a successful franchise.

Scary offerings included the odd but successful *Gremlins (*1984) directed by Joe Dante, and Stanley Kubrick's very scary *The Shining* (1980). Comedy was highlighted by the excellent *Trading Places* (1983) directed by John Landis – marked out by very good acting and a first class script. Eddie Murphy, who co-starred with Dan Ackroyd in this, also featured in the *Beverly Hills Cop* franchise (1984, 1987 and 1994). Other fun comedies of the time included *Police Academy* (1984) directed by Hugh Wilson, *Ghostbusters* (1984) directed by Ivan Reitman, *Airplane!* (1980), written and directed by David Zucker, Jim Abrahams and Jerry Zucker, along with the sequel *Airplane 2: The Sequel* (1982) directed by Ken Finkleman, and Peter Faiman's *Crocodile Dundee* (1986) starring Paul Hogan.

There were some films that have become classics: *Tootsie* (1982) directed by the wonderful Sydney Pollack and starring Dustin Hoffman, Ridley Scott's excellent *Blade Runner*, *Sophie's Choice* (1982) directed by Alan Pakula, Peter Weir's *Witness* (1985), *Beetlejuice* (1988) directed by Tim Burton and *Big* (1988) directed by Penny Marshall. Adrian Lyne directed the disturbing but very sexy *9½ Weeks* (1986) and Barry Levinson gave us *Good Morning Vietnam* (1987) starring Robin Williams. *Who Framed Roger Rabbit* (1988) directed by Robert Zemeckis mixed live action and animation material. *Rain Man* (1988), directed by Barry Levinson, was brilliant as was *When Harry Met Sally* (1989) directed by Rob Reiner. Barry Levinson's *The Natural* (1984) and Phil Alden Robinson's *Field of Dreams* (1989), both about baseball, were truly inspirational as were *Driving Miss Daisy* (1989) directed by Bruce Beresford and *Dead Poets Society* (1989) directed by Peter Weir.

Woody Allen's offerings included *Stardust Memories* (1980), *Zelig* (1983), *Broadway Danny Rose* (1984), *The Purple Rose of Cairo* (1985), *Hannah and Her Sisters* (1986), *Radio Days* (1987) and *Crimes and Misdemeanors* (1989). From the UK stable, we had Hugh Hudson's *Chariots of Fire* (1981), *Gandhi* (1982) directed by Richard Attenborough, the very disturbing and erotic *The Draughtsman's Contract* (1983) directed by Peter Greenaway and the deliberately shocking, black comedy *The Cook, the Thief, His Wife & Her Lover* (1989) also directed by Greenaway. *Highlander* (1986) directed by Russell Mulcahy started a franchise and the quirkily brilliant *Withnail & I* (1987) directed by Bruce Robinson started a cult. Three films telling good stories from Terry Gilliam were *Time Bandits* (1981), *Brazil* (1985) and *The Adventures of Baron Munchausen* (1988). In all, the 1980s offered visual and filmic treats with very powerful inspirational elements worthy of recall. Let's see.

FROM THE PLAY

49 EDUCATING RITA

WRITTEN BY WILLY RUSSELL (1980)

This play, commissioned by the UK's Royal Shakespeare Company, was made into a film in 1983, starring Michael Caine and Julie Walters. It was adapted by Russell and directed by Lewis Gilbert. Exploring ideas of class, education, snobbery, freedom, change, the shortcomings of institutional education, the nature of self-development and of personal relationships, it is funny in parts and passionately inspiring in others.

THE STORY

Rita, a Liverpudlian hairdresser pursuing a course in English Literature, meets her tutor, Dr Frank Bryant, for the first time. The two are seemingly very different, one working class, bright but poorly educated and the other, sorry for and bored with himself, life's mores and life itself. But Frank is impressed by Rita and by her keen willingness to learn. He begins to look at his own life afresh. Rita marvels at Frank's knowledge and the fact that he can open doors for her to a new environment. She grows in confidence. However, as the relationship of understanding grows, Frank returns to his bitter stance as he sees Rita, who now trendily wants to be known as Susan, behaving in a pretentious way that he despises. Susan is badly affected by the suicide attempt of a friend and begins to understand that the new culture that she's embraced is in fact superficial. Frank is obliged to go to Australia on a sabbatical at the play's end for drunken behaviour. We're not sure whether Susan goes with him, but we'd like to think she does.

THE SPEECH

This extract is well into the play when Rita has begun to appreciate literature fully. The simple dialogue is inspirational. We see hope and aspiration in her and support and understanding from Frank. The dialogue is innocent and touching:

"Susan: Er, excuse me a moment. Frank, Frank, I'm sorry, I just had to tell somebody.

Frank: What's wrong?

Susan: Last night, Frank, I went to the theatre.

Frank: I thought it was something serious!

Susan: It was. It was Shakespeare!

Frank: I thought something happened to you.

Susan: Something did happen to me. It was fantastic. Macbeth, it was. I bought the book!

Oh, it done my head in. I thought it was gonna be dead boring, but it wasn't, it was electric. Wasn't his wife a cow? And that bit where he meets Macduff and thinks he's all invincible. I was on the edge of me seat because I knew! I wanted to shout out and warn Macbeth!

Frank: You didn't, did you?

Susan: No! They'd have thrown me out the theatre. Macbeth's a tragedy, isn't it?

Frank: Right.

Susan: Right. Well, I... I just wanted to tell someone who'd understand.

Frank: Rita, I am honoured that you chose me."

FROM THE PLAY

50 THE LIFE AND ADVENTURES OF NICHOLAS NICKLEBY

ADAPTED AND WRITTEN BY DAVID EDGAR

This eight-hour play, adapted and written by David Edgar from the Dickens' novel (1839) of the same title, was first directed by Trevor Nunn and John Caird. It was revived by the Royal Shakespeare Company (RSC) in 1986 where it enjoyed a second superb run. Dramatic triumphs such as this rarely come along.

THE STORY

Young Nicholas, along with his mother and sister Kate, are left penniless by the death of Nicholas' father and are forced to seek financial assistance from the boy's uncle, Ralph Nickleby. Ralph, a usurer, sends Nicholas to teach at Dotheboys Hall, which is run by sadistic schoolmaster Wackford Squeers, who delights in savagely beating his charges – aided and abetted by his son, daughter and wife. Nicholas, unable to stand any more cruelty, thrashes the evil Squeers and escapes the school with Smike, a wretched, lame and ill boy the school has badly abused. Eventually Nicholas saves Kate from the attentions and insults of Sir Mulberry Hawk (a wealthy bully) and continuously protects Smike, while trying to stop his Uncle Ralph taking advantage of his sister Kate and later his sweetheart, Madeline Bray, whose father is in a debtors' prison. Ralph gets his comeuppance when it is discovered that Smike is his son. Ralph's disgrace is too much and he commits suicide and, although Smike dies of consumption, there is a general sense of justice and happiness at the story's close.

THE SPEECH

Newman Noggs, Ralph Nickleby's clerk, is destined to become Nicholas' greatest friend. Watching Ralph's criminal schemes has driven him to continued drinking and he wrings his hands constantly in frustration. When he overhears Ralph plotting to trade Madeline for releasing a debtor's debts, Noggs is horrified and is pushed into action. Noggs becomes a kind of father to Nicholas as he urges the young man to overturn the plan and marry Madeline himself. Early in the narrative when Nicholas is in the depths of despondency at Dotheboys Hall, he receives a letter from Noggs. Onstage, Noggs speaks his letter as we see Nicholas read it:

"My dear young man. I know the world. Your father did not, or he would not have done me a kindness when there was no hope of return. You do not, or would not be bound on such a journey. If ever you want shelter in London, they know where I live at the sign of the Crown, in Silver St., Golden Square. You can come at night. Once, nobody was ashamed – never mind that. It's all over. Excuse errors. I have forgotten all my old ways. My spelling may have gone with them.

Nicholas (reads): Yours obediently, Newman Noggs.

Noggs: PS. If you should go near Barnard Castle, there is good ale at the King's Head. Say you know me and I am sure they will not charge you for it. You may say Mr. Noggs there, for I was a gentleman then. I was indeed."

The speech, the letter, brings Nicholas to tears. Here is such inherent decency and kindness in a Dickensian world where little existed. Here is an example of humility and we must really cherish writing where humility is borne out and inspires us.

FROM THE FILM

51 RAIDERS OF THE LOST ARK

DIRECTED BY STEVEN SPIELBERG (1981)

Produced by George Lucas, this is the first film in a franchise and stars a magnificent Harrison Ford. The storyline pits Indiana Jones against the Nazis who are trying to find the Biblical Ark of the Covenant so that the German army can become immortal. The film allegedly cost about $18m to make and by late 1982 had grossed over $230m in the US alone. It won four Academy Awards.

THE STORY

Indiana Jones is an archeologist who manages to get into all sorts of adventures in the pursuit of his profession. He hears from museum curator Marcus Brody (Denhom Elliott) about a biblical artifact called The Ark of the Covenant, which apparently contains the original Ten Commandments, and is asked by the US Government to seek out the Ark before the Nazis get hold of it. Jones must battle Renee Belloq (Paul Freeman) who's paid by the Nazis to find the Ark.

Amidst dangers galore, Indy and old flame Marion (Karen Allen), aided by the faithful and knowledgeable Dr Brody, chase the Germans and the Ark. The action moves fast and furiously, with the Ark eventually ending up on an island, where Belloq opens it. When he does, demons and angels of death are released and kill all who behold them. Luckily the good guys have their eyes closed.

The last shot is powerful. We see the Ark now in a huge wooden crate and the camera pulls back to reveal a warehouse full of many other huge wooden crates. Are these other religious artifacts?

THE SPEECH

Among the many inspirational moments, some key ones get the blood racing. These are moments when you know you're in with the good who are not yet winning against the bad, but you know they will.

“Jones (excitedly): The Nazis have discovered Tanis ... Tanis is one of the possible resting places of the Lost Ark ... the Ark of the Covenant, the chest the Hebrews used to carry around the Ten Commandments in ... the original stone tablets that Moses brought down … and smashed ... The Hebrews took the broken pieces and put them in the Ark. When they settled in Canaan, they put the Ark in … the Temple of Solomon … where it stayed for many years, until, all of a sudden, whoosh, it was gone ... Nobody knows where or when.

Brody: However, an Egyptian pharaoh Shishak invaded the city of Jerusalem around about 980 BC and he may have taken the Ark back to the city of Tanis and hidden it in a secret chamber called the Well of Souls ... However, about a year after the pharaoh had returned to Egypt, the city of Tanis was consumed by the desert in a sandstorm which lasted a whole year, wiped clean by the wrath of God ...

Agent: What does this Ark look like?"

Our necks tingle. Indiana Jones pulls out a book, flips through the pages and finds a large dramatic drawing showing the Israelite army vanquishing a foe. Hebrew priests carry the beautiful Ark of the Covenant. From the side of the Ark held high above the battle, the drawing shows a brilliant sheet of fire and something very powerful.

FROM THE FILM

52 GANDHI

DIRECTED BY RICHARD ATTENBOROUGH (1982)

The film, a vast biopic about Mahatma Gandhi, starred Ben Kingsley and won eight Academy Awards.

THE STORY

This account of the Indian political activist's life starts with Gandhi being shot by an assassin, followed by a scene with thousands of mourners. We then go back in time and find Gandhi as a young, principled lawyer in South Africa riding on a train. Although he holds a first-class ticket, he's ordered to go to third-class because of his status as a minority. He refuses and is thrown off.

Gandhi is inspired to create equality and bring an end to racial oppression. He returns to India where he attempts to bring change to the Indian people, but the paranoid British authorities jail him repeatedly. Gandhi grows increasingly frustrated as violence on both sides escalates. He eventually goes on a hunger strike after a brutal mass murder of peaceful Indian protestors and does the same again after witnessing struggles between Hindus and Muslims and between Indians in general and the British. We see the continual rise of a non-violent philosopher-leader commanding respect (and eventually from all sides).

THE SPEECH

"When I despair, I remember that all through history the ways of truth and love have always won. There have been tyrants and murderers and, for a time they can seem invincible, but in the end they always fall. Think of it – always."

This is Gandhi's voiceover (Ben Kingsley's) at the very end of the film as we see Gandhi's ashes scattered over the River Ganges. The paragraph sums up the spirit of the man and, whether one agrees with his politics or not, the small speech puts into context the huge influence Gandhi had (and still has) over a vast country.

FROM THE FILM

53 THE WALL

DIRECTED BY ALAN PARKER (1982)

Rock opera *The Wall* is based on the Pink Floyd album of the same name. The film is a mixture of live action and Gerald Scarfe animation. It features some now memorable Pink Floyd songs and the album still sells extraordinarily well.

THE STORY

Pink (Bob Geldoff), a depressed rock star, is in a hotel and has totally destroyed his room. We learn that Pink's father was killed during World War II when Pink was small. There's a flashback to Pink as a child when he needed a father. To compensate, his mother (Christine Hargreaves) is very protective. At school he is tormented for being something of a romantic and a teacher humiliates him for writing poetry.

Pink gets married, but his wife (Eleanor David) has an affair while he's on tour. Gradually, Pink goes mad. Trapped by success and loneliness, he hides within a self-imposed wall. Pink's manager (Bob Hoskins) and hotel manager (Michael Ensign) find him in a comatose state and a doctor gives him drugs so he can perform onstage at a gig. Pink hallucinates, believing himself to be a neo-Nazi dictator and his concert is, he thinks, a huge rally. His followers in turn attack minorities. We're not sure how much of this is imagined or real. Pink stops his erratic behaviour and puts himself on (we assume imaginary) trial, the result of which is that the wall is torn down. The film ends with a shot of the debris and children playing in ruins. The closing moment is a freeze on one of the children emptying a petrol bomb. We never find out what happened to Pink.

THE SPEECH

There is a scene where Pink's manager and hotel staff find Pink unconscious in his room. A doctor administers an injection which will revitalise Pink. What follows is a song, *Comfortably Numb*, the tune and lyrics of which combine to inspire. Hugely. The ingredients mix and deliver a gulp moment where we want Pink to get up and perform. This song is one of Pink Floyd's most famous, with superb guitar solos performed by Dave Gilmour.

It begins with the doctor singing "Hello, is there anybody in there? …" Pink responds by singing, "There is no pain you are receding …" and finishing with "I have become comfortably numb".

The music soars as do our spirits. For the moment at least, we're safe, comfortably numb. That's reassuring and is a lift.

FROM THE FILM

54 BLADE RUNNER

DIRECTED BY RIDLEY SCOTT (1982)

This was a very different film from the usual sci-fi fare. The film shows a frightening and dark image of Los Angeles in 2019, where robots called replicants (looking exactly like humans) abound. It stars Harrison Ford whose job it is to find and destroy the replicants which have become dangerous. The film has become a classic with a number of different cuts available to its ever-growing number of fans. Its screenplay was based on science-fiction writer Philip K. Dick's 1968 novel, *Do Androids Dream of Electric Sheep?*

THE STORY

Technology in the not so distant future has allowed us to build robots (human clones) to serve outside Earth on its colonies. These replicants have fixed life spans in case they become too human. Rick Deckard (Harrison Ford), a recently retired Blade Runner – a specialist police officer whose job is replicant termination – is forced to take up his job once again when some replicants escape from a colony and return to Earth to find their creator and force him to prolong their lives.

This theme of seeking immortality is the crux of the film as is the philosophical question as to what constitutes a human being. The film also pinpoints the preciousness of life.

THE SPEECH

The film is inspiring in its illustration of the fact that the human condition is one to safeguard and cherish. Is it too late already? Will robots, humanoid in all details, one day have the sort of power which now draws a smirk from us?

The final vivid and brutal chase scene between Roy Batty (Rutger Hauer) and Deckard onto a rooftop is powerful and, because we know we're near the end, tense. Deckard is rescued from the edge of the building, following which we get Batty's climactic, mournful and poignant soliloquy:

> “I've seen things you people wouldn't believe. Attack ships on fire off the shoulder of Orion. I watched c-beams glitter in the dark near Tanhauser Gate. All those moments will be lost in time like tears in rain. Time to die ...”

His robotic life expires in the rain and a white dove flies upward – supplemented by Deckard narrating at the film's finish:

> “I don't know why he saved my life. Maybe in those last moments he loved life more than he ever had before. Not just his life – anybody's life; my

life. All he'd wanted were the same answers the rest of us want. Where did I come from? Where am I going? How long have I got? All I could do was sit there and watch him die."

The sequences are inspirational. There is hope and an acknowledgement that, no matter what, compassion and humanity are key to survival. But, the whole film is deliciously ambiguous, not least as to whether or not the Blade Runner himself is a replicant ...

FROM THE FILM

55 TOOTSIE

DIRECTED BY SYDNEY POLLACK (1982)

This hugely enjoyable comedy has a tight script, a great storyline, superb actors (particularly Dustin Hoffman) and is brilliantly directed. Its premise is simple: a resting actor, with a reputation for being difficult, decides to disguise himself as a woman to get a role in a TV soap opera. We see something similar in the later and equally excellent *Mrs. Doubtfire* (1993) directed by Chris Columbus.

THE STORY

Michael Dorsey (Hoffman), an unemployed actor, dresses as a woman to become Dorothy Michaels and lands a lead role, Emily Kimberley, a no-nonsense administrator, in a daytime TV hospital drama, Southwest General. He inspires women all over the place to break free from men and meanwhile falls for co-star Julie (Jessica Lange) while her father (Charles Durning) falls for him (as Dorothy).

After many confusing and delightful scenarios, all ends well. Michael has left the soap. Julie admits that she misses Dorothy, but Michael quickly reminds her that he *is* Dorothy but "I just gotta learn to do it without the dress".

THE SPEECH

Among the many inspiring elements of the film, two particular moments come to mind. One is where Michael is arguing with his agent George about the fact that nobody wants to hire him as an actor anymore because he has a reputation for being difficult. It's a wonderfully funny and wry scene and sets in context what's to follow:

“Michael Dorsey: Are you saying that nobody in New York will work with me?

George Fields: No, no, that's too limited ... nobody in Hollywood wants to work with you either. I can't even set you up for a commercial. You played a tomato for 30 seconds – they went a half a day over schedule because you wouldn't sit down.

Michael Dorsey: Of course. It was illogical.

George Fields: You were the tomato! A tomato doesn't have logic. A tomato can't move.

Michael Dorsey: That's what I said. So if he can't move, how's he gonna sit down, George? I was a stand-up tomato: a juicy, sexy, beefsteak tomato. Nobody does vegetables like me. I did an evening of vegetables off-Broadway. I did the best tomato, the best cucumber ... I did an endive salad that knocked the critics on their ass.”

The other scene is when Michael goes as Dorothy for a screen-test for a role in the soap. He's with director Ron Carlisle:

“Ron Carlisle: I'm afraid you're not right for this role. Thanks for coming by.

Dorothy: Why am I not right, Mister Carlisle?

Ron Carlisle: I'm trying to make a certain statement and I'm looking for a specific physical type.

Dorothy: Mr. Carlisle, I'm an actress. I'm a character actress. I can play it any way you want.

Ron Carlisle: I'm sure you're a very good actress. It's just that you're not threatening enough.

Dorothy: Not threatening enough? Listen, you take your hands off me or I'll knee your balls right through the roof of your mouth! Is that enough of a threat?

Ron Carlisle [shaken]: It's a start.”

Don't we wish we could sometimes get away with saying things like that? And, if we can't, isn't it inspirational witnessing someone else do it?

FROM THE FILM

56 THE RIGHT STUFF

DIRECTED BY PHILIP KAUFMAN (1983)

Adapted by Kaufman from Tom Wolf's 1979 book of the same name, this film is about the early years of the American space programme. It won four Academy Awards and was eminent in pioneering film sound and visual effects.

THE STORY

The film covers the true story of the breaking of the sound barrier in 1947 by test pilot Chuck Yeager (Sam Shepard). Then it's 1953 and a group of test pilots are edging closer to space and going ever faster. We get to understand more about the tensions between pilots and wives at home. Each test could be the last for a pilot and, because the flights are at the edge of what's possible, the real chance of tragedy is ever present.

The Russians' launching of the Sputnik satellite throws the US space training programme into overdrive. Yeager isn't allowed to be a space pilot because he doesn't have an academic qualification. From the really hard and harsh competition to find the right astronauts, only a few emerge to be part of what was called the Mercury 7 programme – John Glenn (Ed Harris), the first American astronaut to orbit the earth and Alan Shepard (Scott Glenn), the first American in space.

The plot covers a fifteen-year period, with a script that is often acerbic, occasionally darkly witty and always sharp. More to the point we get to understand why all the pilots had the right stuff and that is really inspirational.

THE SPEECH

Of the many hugely moving and inspirational moments and scenes within the film, two count for much: one where nervous humour sums up the risk factor. Yes, this is merely a movie, but it's about real people.

> "Alan Shepard: Dear Lord, please don't let me fuck up.
> Gordon Cooper: I didn't quite copy that. Say again, please.
> Alan Shepard: I said everything's A-OK."

The other moment is at the very end of the film when we hear the voiceover declaring what's happened. We have been inspired by bravery and loss, losing and winning, by evidence of pioneers who are on par with any of history's other pioneers:

"The Mercury programme was over. Four years later, astronaut Gus Grissom was killed, along with astronauts White and Chaffee, when fire swept through their Apollo capsule. But on that glorious day in May 1963, Gordo Cooper went higher, farther and faster than any other American – twenty two complete orbits around the world; he was the last American ever to go into space alone. And for a brief moment, Gordo Cooper became the greatest pilot anyone had ever seen."

Consider for a long moment. Consider.

FROM THE FILM

57 WITHNAIL & I

DIRECTED BY BRUCE ROBINSON (1986)

This classic film starring Richard E. Grant (as Withnail) and Paul McGann (as Marwood) has taken on cult status and is watched and quoted freely by each successive generation.

THE STORY

There's not much on the horizon for two out-of-work actors and they have little money, so they decide to leave their drink and drug-fuelled squalid existence in London and go for a refreshing holiday in the country – to stay at Withnail's uncle Monty's cottage. When they arrive, it's cold and wet and, worse, there's no food. The two find it hard to survive. Uncle Monty (Richard Griffiths) then arrives with supplies and takes a shine to Marwood.

A telegram arrives for Marwood inviting him to audition for a part in a play. The two actors return to London where Marwood discovers he's actually in line to play the lead in the play for which he's auditioning. He goes off to the station in the rain with an unwelcome Withnail accompanying him part of the way.

THE SPEECH

At the end of the film, Withnail quotes from Shakespeare's *Hamlet* (Act II, scene 2) to wolves in London Zoo while standing in the rain and drinking from a wine-bottle:

"… I have of late – but wherefore I know not – lost all my mirth, forgone all custom of exercises; and indeed it goes so heavily with my disposition that this goodly frame, the earth, seems to me a sterile promontory, this most excellent canopy, the air, look you, this brave o'erhanging firmament, this majestical roof fretted with golden fire, why, it appears no other thing to me than a foul and pestilent congregation of vapours. What a piece of work is a man! How noble in reason! How infinite in faculty! In form and moving how express and admirable! In action how like an angel! In apprehension how like a god! The beauty of the world! The paragon of animals! And yet, to me, what is this quintessence of dust? Man delights not me: no, nor woman neither …"

This speech, with its poignant and poetic descriptions, is a great example of Hamlet's eloquence and it's this that creates inspiration, not just in the play itself, but in the situation in which Withnail now finds himself – friendless and lost in life. Like Hamlet, Withnail is disillusioned, but we get buoyed up by the fact that his friend will be fine and actually he might be too. He makes the speech sound positive and elegant. We think that maybe he's auditioning perhaps and the wolves in the zoo seem to approve. As do we.

FROM THE FILM

58 RADIO DAYS

DIRECTED BY WOODY ALLEN (1987

This film, in which director Woody Allen also stars, is a pleasantly sentimental, comedic reminiscence about the 1940s – the golden age of radio. Allen's love for his subject, the romantic nostalgia he feels, translates seamlessly to the screen. Whatever one thinks of Allen and his work, it's important to note that he's won three Academy Awards and been nominated many times: fourteen as a screenwriter, six as a director and one as an actor.

THE STORY

There isn't a proper story as such; the film is more an amalgam of various parts brought very loosely together. There isn't a true ending either. What we get is a slice of life, a series of moments beautifully observed. The narrator (Woody Allen) tells the audience how radio has affected and influenced his life, particularly before the advent of television. We hear about the radio stars of the Forties.

Each member of the narrator's New York Jewish family escapes into the world of radio, whether that be via sportsmen and sports programme hosts, singers, celebrities or quiz programme MCs. It's like a parallel world. The narrator is inspired, as are we, by the adventures of caped and masked avengers and other action-packed stories. We also learn about Sally (Mia Farrow) and her rise from cigarette seller to radio. She's sweet. "Who is Pearl Harbor?" she asks in genuine confusion on 7 December 1941. In tandem, we're treated to details of the narrator's Aunt Bea (Dianne Wiest) and her madcap and funny, romantic adventures.

The script is typically Woody Allen – well-observed moments, a warm view of a particular cloying New York Jewish family and the way people identify with media moments. The humour is light but crisp and fun; the soundtrack on its own – the voiceover, the music, the dialogue – would make a great radio programme in its own right.

THE SPEECH

Of the various high points, one particularly inspiring moment is towards the end and in the narrator's moving and gentle monologue. This is Allen being Allen at his best and we certainly get the feeling that it's from the author's heart. The piece is in voiceover as he recalls 1943's New Year's Eve:

> "I never forgot that New Year's Eve when Aunt Bea awakened me to watch 1944 come in. And I've never forgotten any of those people or any of the voices we used to hear on the radio. Although the truth is ... with the passing of each New Year's Eve, those voices do seem to grow dimmer and dimmer."

If you haven't seen this film, go and watch it. If you have, refresh yourself and be inspired yet again.

FROM THE FILM

59 THE LAST EMPEROR

DIRECTED BY BERNARDO BERTOLUCCI (1987)

This lavish biopic about the life of Puyi, the last Emperor of China, begins with Puyi ascending the throne as a small boy and finishes with his imprisonment and political rehabilitation by the Chinese Communists. The film won nine Academy Awards including Best Picture and Best Director.

THE STORY

In 1950 Puyi is being introduced as a war criminal into the new People's

Republic of China. He tries to commit suicide but fails. We see a flashback to his childhood and first experiences of the Forbidden City. We witness his treatment as a deity, his upbringing, education, development, the politics and power of his time. It is extraordinary and illuminating. We also see the development of the Chinese Republic, the emperor's exile and his eventual capture by the Russians. Interwoven into the film are flash forward scenes of his captivity and prison life. The contrasts between the squalor of this existence and his former glory are immense.

At the film's end, the period of China's Cultural Revolution, a reformed Puyi has been released and is now a simple gardener. He sees a huge parade celebrating Mao and notices his prison chief being punished for insufficient revolutionary zeal. Puyi visits the Forbidden City – he wants to see his old throne, but a little boy – part of the Mao Pioneer Movement – tries to stop him. The boy is persuaded that Puyi is indeed the previous emperor and Puyi sits on his old throne. He finds the sixty-year old cricket he kept as a child and gives it to the boy, who wants to thank Puyi, but the former Emperor has gone.

The film ends with a tour guide leading a group in front of the throne. The guide explains Puyi's life in a few short, matter-of-fact sentences, which include the date of his death. It is heartbreaking.

THE SPEECH

Especially for those who know little of imperial China, the film is an eye-opener, with huge contrasts. There are moving scenes and uplifting ones in equal measure. The inspirational moments are those when we see once again that mankind is harsh on mankind. And there are touching moments. This one is a brief exposition given by the Emperor's tutor, Reginald Fleming Johnston (Peter O'Toole):

"The Emperor has been a prisoner in his own palace since the day that he was crowned, and has remained a prisoner since he abdicated. But now he's growing up, he may wonder why he's the only person in China who may not walk out of his own front door. I think the Emperor is the loneliest boy on Earth."

FROM THE FILM

60 BIG

DIRECTED BY PENNY MARSHALL (1988)

If I had to prioritise some of the films in this book, this would be in my top ten. It's funny, (very) clever, witty, charming, heart-warming and has a great story – about a boy who makes a wish at a fairground fortune-telling machine to be big. Overnight, he ages and grows. Tom Hanks stars, showing real understanding of a child behaving like a man. Elizabeth Perkins as Susan, the love interest, is superb. *Big* was made into a Broadway musical in 1996.

THE STORY

Josh Baskin makes a wish at a fortune-telling machine. He wants to be big so he can go on a fairground ride. The next day he looks like a man of thirty, but still with the mannerisms and behaviour of a twelve-year-old. He runs away to New York to find the fortune-telling machine to unmake his wish, accompanied by his best friend Billy (Jared Rushton) who knows what's happened. In New York, Josh meets a toy company owner, MacMillan (Robert Loggia) in a toy shop and the two play a famous duet of *Chopsticks* on a giant floor piano. MacMillan employs Josh to test toys, which is, of course, a brilliant job for a twelve-year-old boy. The lovely Susan likes Josh and a slightly one-sided romance blooms, although Susan's boyfriend (John Heard) is none too pleased. Billy also feels left out as Josh wants to spend more time in his new adult world.

Josh is asked to suggest a new line of toys and begins to find this executive pressure too much. Soon he wants to get back to his previous life. Billy finds out that the fortune-telling machine is back and Josh rushes off just as he's making a pitch to the MacMillan management team about his new toy line – which will, or would be, a surefire hit. Susan secretly follows Josh who makes the wish to revert to his original self. Susan now realises that the relationship has nowhere to go although Josh tells her how important she has been to him. She takes Josh home.

The brilliant angle of the film is that we love the idea of an adult being able to keep the innocence and excitement of the child. That alone is inspirational – not least because of a great script and great acting.

THE SPEECH

While the whole film is inspirational and heart-warming, there are moments when the heart is made warmer still. Take, for example, when Mrs. Baskin, Josh's mother, is talking to Josh thinking he's her son's kidnapper:

> “Mrs. Baskin: You have my son?
>
> Josh [over the phone]: Yes.
>
> Mrs. Baskin: Look, if you touch one hair on his head, I swear I will spend the rest of my life making sure you suffer.
>
> Josh: Wow, thanks.”

Or when Josh has started work at the toy company and one of his new colleagues is inducting Josh into the way of the business:

> “Scotty Brennan: See that girl over there in the red? Say hi to her and she's yours. She'll have her legs around you so tight you'll be begging for mercy.
>
> Josh: Well, I'll stay away from her, then.”

The film ends with a poignant final shot of Susan seeing Josh, after saying and waving goodbye, transformed into a boy again, with the grown-up suit that now doesn't fit him. He runs into his home shouting: “Mom? ... I missed you all so much.” A short epilogue shows Josh and Billy walking down the street discussing playing stick ball.

FROM THE FILM

61 THE FIELD OF DREAMS

DIRECTED BY PHIL ALDEN ROBINSON (1989)

This moving and, in parts, hugely inspirational film, starring Kevin

Costner, is based on the novel, *Shoeless Joe* by W.P. Kinsella published in 1982.

THE STORY

Farmer Ray Kinsella (Kevin Costner) hears a voice in his cornfield which says, "If you build it, he will come". Ray interprets the odd message as an instruction to build a baseball pitch in the middle of a cornfield on his farm. Which he does.

The voices continue and so a bemused Ray seeks out a faded author, Terence Mann (James Earl Jones), to help him understand the meaning of the messages and the purpose of his field. At first, it seems the person for whom he's supposed to be waiting is the ghost of long gone, disgraced baseball player, Shoeless Joe Jackson (Ray Liotta), who materialises on the field and plays a few games with an amazed and then delighted Ray. Ray receives other messages from a disembodied voice, one of which is "Ease his pain". He realises that his baseball field has been earmarked by someone or something to give people who have made sacrifices in their lives a second chance at baseball. One of these people is Doc Graham (Burt Lancaster in his last role), a beloved general practitioner who gave up a brilliant baseball career in favour of medicine. People from miles around visit the baseball field in the hope of seeing something extraordinary. We are inspired by the faith the film reinforces, the look and the smile, the hope that humanity is on the whole decent. The final ghost turns out to be much closer to Ray – his father – and that reunion really gets the tears going. Anyone who has ever played catch with his (or indeed her) father will be very touched by this story.

THE SPEECH

One of the inspirational moments is when reclusive and down-at-heel author Terence Mann gives a moving "People will come" speech to Ray. It is powerful rhetoric about how baseball fits into the American psyche and designed to help Ray understand the voices and the reason for the baseball field:

"... People will come, Ray. They'll come to Iowa for reasons they can't even fathom ... They'll arrive at your door, as innocent as children, longing for the past ... They'll pass over the money without even thinking about it: for it is money they have and peace they lack ... And they'll walk off to the bleachers and sit in their short sleeves on a perfect afternoon ... And they'll watch the game and it'll be as if they'd dipped themselves in magic waters ... People will come, Ray ...The one constant through all the years, Ray, has been baseball ... This field, this game, is a part of our past, Ray. It reminds us of all that once was good and that could be again ... people will come, Ray. People will most definitely come..."

And we let the tears roll quietly at the kind words and the sentiment behind them.

FROM THE FILM

62 HENRY V

DIRECTED BY KENNETH BRANNAGH (1989)

This film in which the director also starred is fresh, strong and far more realistic than Laurence Olivier's version in 1944. Based on Shakespeare's play of power and war, it examines the king and his personality more so than many stage productions. Brannagh stresses the emotional elements, in particular, the major rhetorical points such as the extraordinarily powerful St. Crispin's Day speech and Mistress Quickly's eulogy for Falstaff.

THE STORY

The Chorus (Derek Jacobi) introduces the play and the young king of England, Henry V, has an angry dialogue with King Charles of France (Paul Scofield). The whole cast is exceptional.

The king's son, the Dauphin (Michael Maloney), insults Henry and that argument leads to war. We see Henry in flashback drinking with Falstaff (Robbie Coltrtrane) in a tavern with the rough, ready and stout-hearted

Bardolph (Richard Briers) along with Nym (Geoffrey Hutchings), Pistol (Robert Stephens) and Mistress Quickly (Judi Dench). Meanwhile, back in the present, Henry and his captain Fluellen (Ian Holm) prepare to invade France. The French outnumber the British troops, but Henry, after delivering the St. Crispin's day speech, leads them to a great victory at Agincourt. Henry woos Katherine of Valois (Emma Thompson), the daughter of Charles VI, and wins her over. (Historically, it was this marriage that enabled Henry to be heir to France.)

At the film's end we go ice cold as we hear the narrator telling us that everything achieved by Henry V would be reversed during his son's reign.

THE SPEECH

Of the many inspirational speeches in this play, there is one perhaps that inspires most: King Henry V's inspired pre-battle address to his weary troops on St. Crispin's Day is simply brilliant:

"This day is called the feast of Crispian:
He that outlives this day, and comes safe home,
Will stand a tip-toe when this day is named,
And rouse him at the name of Crispian.
He that shall see this day and live old age,
Will yearly on the vigil feast his neighbours,
And say 'To-morrow is Saint Crispin's'
Then will he strip his sleeve and show his scars.
And say 'These wounds I had on Crispin's day.'
Old men forget: yet all shall be forgot,
But he'll remember with advantages
What feats he did that day.
Then shall our names,
Familiar in their mouths as household words,
Harry the king,
Bedford and Exeter,
Warwick and Talbot,

Salisbury and Gloucester,
Be in their flowing cups freshly remember'd.
This story shall the good man teach his son;
And Crispin Crispian shall ne'er go by,
From this day to the ending of the world,
But we in it shall be remember'd;
We few, we happy few, we band of brothers;
For he to-day that sheds his blood with me
Shall be my brother; be he ne'er so vile,
This day shall gentle his condition:
And gentlemen in England now a-bed
Shall think themselves accursed they were not here,
And hold their manhoods cheap whiles any speaks
That fought with us upon Saint Crispin's day.”

Saint Crispin's Day falls on 25 October and is the feast day of the Christian saints Crispin and Crispinian, twins who were martyred circa A.D. 286. Elements of this speech are often used to urge people (not just armies) to action. Read it aloud. Go on.

FROM THE FILM

63 WHEN HARRY MET SALLY

DIRECTED BY ROB REINER (1989)

Written by Nora Ephron, this delightful film is warm, episodic, sharp, witty, engaging and has a big dollop of inspiration at its heart. It's beautifully observed and follows a long-term hot/cold relationship between the two protagonists over a twelve-year period. We want it and Harry (Billy Crystal) and Sally (Meg Ryan) to work.

THE STORY

Harry Burns and Sally Albright meet in late 1970 as they drive together to

New York City after college. They bicker about friendships between men and women claiming that sex interferes. After a five-year gap they meet again and still don't get on particularly well. Another six years pass and Harry has been married, but is now getting divorced. Sally has split up with her long-term boyfriend. Now they do become friends and they have sex, but that changes the relationship, as they always thought it would. It all ends happily ever after though, exactly as *we* always hoped it would.

THE SPEECH

The whole film is uplifting and the writing is clever and bang on the money. Harry's "why I love you" speech to Sally at a New Year's Eve party towards the film's end particularly hits the spot:

> "... I love that you get cold when it's 71 degrees out. I love that it takes you an hour and a half to order a sandwich. I love that you get a little crinkle in your nose when you're looking at me like I'm nuts. I love that after I spend day with you, I can still smell your perfume on my clothes. And I love that you are the last person I want to talk to before I go to sleep at night. And it's not because I'm lonely, and it's not because it's New Year's Eve. I came here tonight because when you realize you want to spend the rest of your life with somebody, you want the rest of your life to start as soon as possible."

From the film

64 BATMAN

Directed by Tim Burton (1989)

This superhero film, based on the DC Comics character of the same name, was the first of a franchise starring Michael Keaton as Batman/Bruce Wayne, Jack Nicholson as The Joker, and Kim Basinger as Vicki Vale.

THE STORY

Bruce Wayne sees his wealthy parents killed when he is a boy. He wants revenge and seeks training from a ninja leader. When he returns, he finds Gotham City decaying and the majority of businesses run by organised crime – mostly led by Carl Grissom (Jack Palance). The company he inherited is being undermined.

Bruce becomes Batman and vows to fight evil and put right any wrong. While raiding a chemical plant, Grissom's second-in-command, Jack Napier (Jack Nicholson), falls into a vat of chemicals which discolours his skin and hair and a bullet disfigures his face. A poor attempt to put him back together again leaves Napier with a fixed grin. Napier kills Grissom and takes control of Gotham's crime industry, but with even more violence. The Joker, as Napier is now called, becomes enchanted by journalist Vicki Vale who is investigating strange bat figure sightings. Batman recognises The Joker as his parents' killer.

The Joker holds a Gotham parade giving out free money, but then plans to gas those who take it. Batman stops the Joker in his tracks, but the Joker kidnaps Vicki. The film ends with the Joker trying to escape from the top of a steeple but, in the altercation, falls to his death. At the very end, a special searchlight projects a bat signal in the sky – whenever he sees the sign, Batman will come to the rescue.

THE SPEECH

There's also a point in most good versus evil stories when we just know that good will win – and that's a satisfying moment. In Batman there's a flashback in which Bruce Wayne remembers his parents being murdered by the man who becomes the Joker – and the killer's chilling line:

> “You ever dance with the devil in the pale moonlight? I always ask that of all my victims!”

It is indeed chilling, but it's also inspirational in that all that surrounds it will come good. We know that the Joker will eventually be in the pale moonlight.

FROM THE FILM

65 DEAD POETS SOCIETY

DIRECTED BY PETER WEIR (1989)

This film, starring Robin Williams, is often omitted when people talk about inspiration. It is about an English teacher played by Williams who inspires his pupils by getting them away from their rigid and pre-set ways of seeing the world. The film won an Academy Award.

THE STORY

It's the late 1950s and Todd Anderson (Ethan Hawke) has just arrived at the smart, expensive school – Welton Academy. He is quiet and shy. His brother was also at the school and extremely successful so he has much to live up to. Todd shares a room with Neil (Robert Sean Leonard) who is popular, but ruled by his bullying father (Kurtwood Smith). New and unconventional teacher Professor Keating (Robin Williams) teaches English to these two and other boys. He gets them to stand on their desks to see the world from a new point of view and also introduces them to the delights of poetry and philosophy. He tells them about the Dead Poets Society and pushes the boys to be bold and revolt against expectations. Neil wants to be an actor and, against his father's wishes, auditions for a part in the school play, *Midsummer Night's Dream*, gets the part of Puck and is really good in it. Neil's father threatens to send him to military school and, in utter despair, the boy commits suicide. Keating takes the blame and loses his job. At the end of the film, though, the boys defend their lost teacher. They have, as teacher Keating says, *carpe diem* – seized the day.

THE SPEECH

There aren't that many films about the love of poetry, so this one particularly appeals to me. Once again we see hope and bravery (eventually) overcome stupidity and narrow mindedness. But not without hurt and tragedy in-between. Keating wants to inspire his charges and does:

"We don't read and write poetry because it's cute. We read and write poetry because we are members of the human race. And the human race is filled with passion. And medicine, law, business, engineering, these are noble pursuits and necessary to sustain life. But poetry, beauty, romance, love, these are what we stay alive for ... the powerful play 'goes on' and you may contribute a verse. What will your verse be?"

AN OVERVIEW OF CHAPTER SIX

During the 1960s and 1970s, Maggie Smith, Ralph Richardson, John Gielgud, Paul Schofield, Michael Bryant, Derek Jacobi and Ian McKellan all delighted and enchanted. Some still do. The sheer depth of voice, character, movement, emotion in any role played by any of these people electrified me. On film the same could be said of James Stewart, Bette Davis, Alistair Sim, Marlon Brando. Here was stage and film that was magical. Magical in that their contributions brought out the psychological, inspirational and emotional truths that their characters demanded.

The Life and Adventures of Nicholas Nickleby was a theatrical experience which lasted more than eight hours. The production received both critical and popular acclaim. Typically Dickensian, it is full of noble, poor people and disreputable rich ones, with complex plotlines that would be the envy of any modern soap. But this is more than mere melodrama and everything (actors, staging, script, sound effects, music, lighting) combined to make it all fresh, exciting and engaging. It's the freshness that is extraordinary. This was theatre at its best, at its most astonishing.

Great films are rare too. And like *The Life and Adventures of Nicholas Nickleby, Raiders of the Lost Ark* has it all, but in different quantities and of a different genre: action, romance, drama, excitement, comedy and suspense. Harrison Ford as Dr. Jones is cool, clever and ingenious but, most of all, human. Steven Spielberg shows off his ability to tell a great, visual good versus evil story. There's also an innocence that is appealing and gratifying.

There's innocence and naivety in Pink Floyd's 1982 film, *The Wall.* Eschewing a traditional narrative, the movie conveys a story through a parade of live-action scenes, both real and imagined, with plenty of brilliant music and surrealist animated segments. At its core, *The Wall* is an analysis of one man's very troubled psyche. It's an intelligent character study that reflects the destructive and unsettling emptiness easily found in modern life. And it's one that sits in the head long, long into the future after the film's end.

Life in the future is the theme of *Blade Runner* and there are ingredients which are ever strong: Vangelis' brooding score, Rutger Hauer's replicant's seminal "I've seen things..." speech, and the extraordinary and believable views of a future LA cityscape. In exploring issues of the "what if" variety, a science fiction universe can have an advantage over a real setting, because it gives writers greater freedom and a larger canvas on which to paint big and speculative questions. *Blade Runner* is also a detective story that adds to continued mental scrutiny. Fear and paranoia is the essence of film noir and this is reflected in the times during which the film was made. Ronald Reagan's own Cold War was underway and the United States was at the tail end of a long economic recession during which time Japan was close to overtaking America as the world's economic superpower. In *Blade Runner*, Japanese businesses and culture have swamped Los Angeles. The lasting impression of the film – depressing but also fascinating – is that the future seems bleak.

Understanding is a common theme in many of the plays and films chosen in this book. When relationships work after not working, the moment of realisation is usually powerful and moving. There are some pieces of art where that moment arrives and uncontrollable weeping is acceptable. In *The Field of Dreams*, there's the moment at the end of this film when the protagonist sees his dead father "alive" again. We all wish that we had another chance to talk to someone with whom that opportunity can never happen. For most, this is a feel-good movie and, for some, it's a reminder that it is never too late to make amends or to have *that* conversation. No, the film isn't about baseball; the sport serves as the backdrop for a story about loss, reconciliation, destiny, redemption, idealism, disappointment, parents, family, dreams and courage.

Henry V is a brilliant story and, of course, most of Shakespeare's plays are great stories brought to vivid comedic, historical or tragic life. This is one of the plays that I remember from visits in 1975 to the RSC in Stratford-upon-Avon when the great Alan Howard played Henry. The play was first performed in 1599 at the Globe Theatre. The story is an intensely simple, sanguine drama of kinghood, bravery and war. It's about a young king's coming of age. In one of Shakespeare's most stirring verbal sonnets, Henry urged his soldiers on to incredible victory – with English deaths at 29 and French with 10,000.

The most inspired part of the play deals with the night before the Battle of Agincourt. No words of any war have yet said what Shakespeare says so honestly or so well. *Henry V* is one of the great experiences in the history of plays and films. It is a major achievement – a perfect marriage of great dramatic poetry with a great contemporary medium for expressing it.

Dramatic poetry features heavily in *Dead Poets Society*. It is a most underrated film by a most underrated director whose inspiring, uplifting and moral tale is firmly grounded in reality and belief. Robin Williams continues in his stride as one who has the ability to measure and deliver touching, heart-wrenching, awe-inspiring emotion and character. His Professor John Keating is a man who embodies every professor whom you thought was decent, kind and respectable, every person who taught or enlightened you in something out of the ordinary.

Chapter Seven

THE 1990s

> "Did you ever reach a point in your life, where you say to yourself: 'This is the best I'm ever going to look, the best I'm ever going to feel, the best I'm ever going to do,' and it ain't that great?" Mitch Robbins (Billy Crystal), *City Slickers* (1991)
>
> "My momma always said, 'Life was like a box of chocolates. You never know what you're gonna get.'" Forrest Gump (Tom Hanks), *Forrest Gump* (1994)

In 1990, Saddam Hussein invaded Kuwait – the United States and a UN coalition force sent troops to defend Kuwait against Iraq. Nelson Mandela was released from prison in South Africa after 28 years and elected president in 1994. East and West Germany were finally reunified and Mikhail Gorbachev was elected president of the Soviet Union. John Major replaced Margaret Thatcher as UK prime minister. In 1991, the US led Operation Desert Storm against Iraq, Boris Yeltsin became Russia's president, PanAm went bust, *The Jerry Springer Show* took to the air and Gorbachev won the 1990 Nobel Peace Prize. 1992 saw the EU becoming an entity, civil war raged in the former Yugoslavia, Windows for PCs (Windows 3.1) was released, the EuroDisney theme park opened in Paris, Bill Clinton became the 42nd US president and *Seinfeld* was a big hit.

In 1993 a huge car bomb exploded at the World Trade Centre in New York, the Intel Pentium chip was launched and the World Wide Web went public. The US fought against Somalia in Mogadishu, the TV series *Frasier* was an immediate hit, as was *The X-Files*. In 1993 Czechoslovakia was dissolved into the Czech Republic and Slovakia. Israeli PM Rabin and Palestinian PM Arafat agreed on a peace process at the Oslo Accords. In 1994 nearly one million people were slaughtered in the Rwandan genocide, the Channel Tunnel opened, the IRA announced a ceasefire, *Friends* became an instant TV hit, Kim Jong-il succeeded Kim Il-sung in North Korea, Barings Bank in the UK was brought down by one broker based in Tokyo and incurred over $1bn in losses. Yahoo! and eBay came into existence. Israeli PM Yitzhak Rabin was assassinated.

The Taliban seized control of Afghanistan in 1996. Gary Kasparov played chess with IBM's supercomputer Deep Blue in 1996 with Kasparov as victor. In 1997, an improved Deep Blue won a rematch and Bill Clinton won a second term. Prince Charles and Princess Diana divorced, Dolly the sheep became the first fully-cloned complex organism, Tony Blair was elected UK Prime Minister, Hong Kong was handed over by the UK to China and Diana, Princess of Wales, was killed in a car accident.

1998 saw Bill Clinton struggling in a sex scandal, Afgahanistan experienced an earthquake which killed 5,000 people and bombs were exploded in Kenya and Tanzania against US embassies. Both Pakistan and India tested nuclear weapons, Google was launched, the first MP3 player was released, the UK TV quiz programme *Who Wants to be a Millionaire?* began and stem cells derived from a human embryo were first isolated. In 1999 Hugo Chavez became Venezuela's president and NATO forces attacked Yugoslavia to prevent further genocide against Albanians. The world went into panic over the Y2K bug. *The Sopranos* hit American TV screens. The Internet saw 295m users and Microsoft was the prime operating system on about 80 per cent of the world's PCs.

The 1990s was the decade of film superstars. Fees earned by top movie actors became epic. The VCR was still a popular appliance in most households and rentals and purchase of videotapes were big business. By 1997, the first DVDs (Digital Video Discs) emerged in shops.

Several film-makers began to use digital imagery, CGI (Computer

Generated Imagery) and DTS (Digital Theatre Systems) to great effect. For example, *Jurassic Park* (1993) and *Twister* (1996) both utilised DTS while *Forrest Gump* (1994) used digital cleverness to insert people into historical footage. George Lucas' *Star Wars Episode I: The Phantom Menace* (1999) included characters that were entirely digitally rendered, such as Jar Jar Binks.

In the world of the novel, we had *Vertigo* by W.G. Sebald in 1990, *The English Patient* by Michael Ondaatje in 1992, Irvine Welsh's *Trainspotting* in 1993, *Angela's Ashes* by Frank McCourt and Chuck Palahniuk's *Fight Club* in 1996, J.K. Rowling's *Harry Potter and the Philosopher's Stone* in 1997 and Joanne Harris' *Chocolat* in 1999. In the world of theatre, we had *Dancing at Lughnasa* (1990) by Brian Friel, *Lettice and Lovage* by Peter Shaffer, *La Bête* (1991), a brilliant comedy set in 17th France by American playwright David Hirson. 1992 saw *Conversations with My Father* from Herb Gardner and *Time of My Life* by Alan Ayckbourn. *Arcadia* was a 1993 play by Tom Stoppard and *My Boy Jack* by David Haig was aired in 1997.

Remarkable (and in many ways inspirational) films of the 1990s included: Tim Burton's *Edward Scissorhands* (1990), Robert Zemeckis' *Back to the Future 3* (1990), Johnathan Demme's *Silence of the Lambs* (1991), Ridley Scott's *Thelma and Louise* (1991), Martin Brest's *Scent of a Woman* (1992), Rob Reiner's *A Few Good Men* (1992), Quentin Tarantino's *Reservoir Dogs* (1992) and *Pulp Fiction* (1994), Chris Columbus' *Mrs. Doubtfire* (1993), Steven Spielberg's *Schindler's List* (1993), Nora Ephron's *Sleepless in Seattle* (1993), Frank Darabont's *The Shawshank Redemption* (1994), Robert Zemeckis' *Forrest Gump* (1994), Michael Radford's *Il Postino* (1995), Danny Boyle's *Trainspotting* (1995), Roberto Benigni's *Life is Beautiful* (1998) and Sam Mendes' *American Beauty* (1999).

Excitement could be found in Martin Scorcese's *Goodfellas* (1990), Oliver Stone's *JFK* (1991), *Speed* (1994) directed by Jan de Bont, *Braveheart* (1995) directed by and starring Mel Gibson, *Apollo 13* (1995) directed by Ron Howard, Michael Mann's *Heat* (1995), Brian de Palma's *Mission: Impossible* (1996), James Cameron's *Titanic* (1997), the fun and witty *Men in Black* (1997) directed by Barry Sonnenfeld, Spielberg's *Saving Private Ryan* (1998), *Star Wars: Episode 1 – The Phantom Menace* (1999) written and directed by George Lucas and *The Matrix* (1999) written and directed by Andy and Larry Wachowski. James Bond also returned in *Golden Eye* (1995) directed by Martin Campbell, *Tomorrow Never Dies* (1997) directed by Roger Spotiswoode and *The World is Not Enough* (1999) directed by Michael Apted.

Animation was offered in the form of *Toy Story* (1995), *Toy Story 2* (1999), *Antz* (1998), *Beauty and the Beast* (1991), Tim Burton's *The Nightmare Before Christmas* (1993) and Disney fare such as *The Lion King* (1994) and *Mulan* (1998). In the realms of comedy, there was Ron Underwood's *City Slickers* (1991), Harold Ramis' *Groundhog Day* (1993), Peter Weir's *The Truman Show* (1998), Mike Newell's *Four Weddings and a Funeral* (1994) and Peter Cattaneo's *The Full Monty* (1997).

Romantic charmers included *Pretty Woman* (1990) directed by Gary Marshall, *Ghost* (1990) directed by Jerry Zucker, Mick Jackson's *The Bodyguard* (1992), James Brooks' *As Good As It Gets* (1997) and John Madden's Shakespearean romance, *Shakespeare in Love* (1998). Let's start with another of my top ten favourites.

FROM THE FILM

66 EDWARD SCISSORHANDS

DIRECTED BY TIM BURTON (1990)

This film, starring Johnny Depp, has pathos, comedy, wit and pace and, most importantly, is a traditional fairy tale. The setting is a dark, gothic castle high on a mountain above a strange suburb of modern America.

THE STORY

Avon lady Pegg Boggs (Dianne Wisest) visits the castle to try and sell cosmetics. She finds a lonely, lost young man called Edward (Johnny Depp) there and takes him home with her. Edward has been made by a crazy inventor (Vincent Price) who has died, leaving the young man alone and unfinished, with scissors for hands and many scars and cuts on his face. At Pegg's home, Edward meets Bill (Alan Arkin) and Kim, the daughter (Winona Ryder).

Initially Edward receives a gentle and warm reception from the neighbours and finds himself absorbed within the quirky community, cutting hair and hedges and eventually creating ice sculptures and snow. Later, loudmouth bully Jim (Anthony Michael Hall) arranges to have a variety of misdemeanours blamed on Edward and sets the town against him. Jim likes Kim who has taken a shine to Edward. When a mob chases Edward, Jim goads Edward into a fight in the gothic castle, but Edward's fingers stab and kill Jim. Kim kisses Edward, then tells the townspeople that both Jim and Edward are dead.

The film ends with an elderly Kim telling her granddaughter (Gina Gallagher) the story of her relationship with Edward Scissorhands, who is still in the castle, still a young man and still creating ice sculptures with his scissorhands. The ice from the sculptures creates snow – something that never happened before Edward's arrival.

THE SPEECH

At the story's end, when we need closure, we get it. The closing monologue by an older Kim Boggs is important when she tells her granddaughter how she knows that Edward Scissorhands is alive and living in the gothic castle. It's a soft and lyrical reflection and that helps us in the process of thinking about our own lives:

> “I don't know. Not for sure. But I believe he is. You see, before he came down here, it never snowed. And afterwards, it did. If he weren't up there now, I don't think it would be snowing. Sometimes ... you can still catch me dancing in it.”

FROM THE FILM

67 JOE VERSUS THE VOLCANO

DIRECTED BY JOHN PATRICK SHANLEY (1990)

This film, which stars Tom Hanks and Meg Ryan, has huge charm and is a fun tale. The palpable chemistry between the two leads is great to see. The film leaves us believing that romance can exist in real life too.

THE STORY

Joe is working for a company that treats its employees with contempt. He has an incurable disease and leaves his dreadful job, packing with him three books: *Robinson Crusoe*, *Romeo and Juliet* and *The Odyssey*. Joe has a date with DeDe (Meg Ryan who also plays two other characters).

A wealthy industrialist named Samuel Graynamore (Lloyd Bridges) makes Joe a proposition. Graynamore's company makes superconductors and needs a special mineral that can be found on a small Pacific island. The islanders will allow mining, but only if Graynamore supplies a human sacrifice – something that the islanders have to do every hundred years. Joe accepts the offer as he feels he has nothing to lose and, in the meantime, can live very well on Graynamore's credit cards.

Joe flies to Los Angeles, where he is met by one of Graynamore's daughters, Angelica (also Ryan). Angelica takes Joe to her father's yacht, captained by her half-sister, Patricia (Ryan again), who reluctantly agrees to take Joe to the Pacific island if she can keep the yacht when she gets back. The yacht is hit by a typhoon and sinks. Joe rescues Patricia, who falls for him after she regains consciousness. They drift towards the island where they are treated to a feast. Patricia tries to stop Joe from being the sacrifice, declaring her love for him. She gets the chief to marry them.

They jump into the volcano together, but at that very moment, it erupts shooting the couple into the sea. The island sinks. On a raft made of Joe's watertight cases, Joe tells Patricia the details of his doctor and illness; she realises that Joe's been the recipient of a big lie. And then it's happy ever after.

THE SPEECH

Joe is adrift in the Pacific with an unconscious Patricia. He's parched and close to madness. He marvels at the beauty of the sea, the sky, the beautiful moon and the equally beautiful Patricia. He bows to the moon, huge and wonderful in the sky, and prays:

"Dear God, whose name I do not know – thank you for my life. I forgot how big ... thank you. Thank you for my life."

FROM THE PLAY

68 LA BÊTE

WRITTEN BY DAVID HIRSON (1991)

Set in 17th century France, this play is loosely styled on Molière's plays. When it opened in Broadway in 1991, it was a flop but when it played in London's West End in 1992, it was very successful, winning the Olivier Award for Best Comedy. Most recently (2010) it has been a terrific hit again in London and on Broadway.

THE STORY

Elomire is a pompous, classical dramatist who loves only the theatre and what he thinks of as pure literature, while Valere is a frivolous street clown and actor who loves only himself. Elomire's main sponsor and patron is the royal princess Conti, but she's grown tired of Elomire's pomposity and quite likes the flamboyant Valere. Elomire and Valere have to pit their different wits for survival as art matches up to ego in a literary showdown. Despite Elomire's violent objections, the company is forced to perform one of Valere's own plays, which results in dramatic changes to the future of Elomire and Valere. Elomire is out on his ear and Valere wins the day.

In the 2010 London production we hear mostly from Valere (Mark Rylance) who, the moment he hits the stage, drinks, eats, spits, picks his teeth, slurs, sniggers at his own cleverness, makes nonsensical boasts and offers equally silly insights into life and literature. Mark Rylance was and is brilliant.

THE SPEECH

The tidal wave of Valere's very long speeches at the beginning of the play starts with a protestation of piety:

> “Devotion comes to nothing if we come to summarise devotion in a sum – a tiny play on words ... Doth please you not? I swear I made it up right on the spot.”

Thirty minutes later he finishes and only because he stuffs a disgusting handkerchief into his own mouth. This opening is a *tour de force*, so powerful that we cannot be but amused, amazed and inspired. Elomire simply can't match the invective and his response sounds relatively limp:

> “Your ignorance is even more colossal – your brain is like some prehistoric fossil.”

If nothing else, read the play.

FROM THE FILM

69 A FEW GOOD MEN

DIRECTED BY ROB REINER (1992)

This film, starring Tom Cruise and Jack Nicholson, is based on the brilliant 1989 play of the same title by Aaron Sorkin. It is about the trial of two US Marines charged with the murder of another Marine and contains one of the most famous lines in movie history: “You can't handle the truth!” spoken by Jack Nicholson's character, Colonel Nathan R. Jessep, to Lieutenant Junior Grade Dan Kaffee played by Tom Cruise.

THE STORY

Daniel Kaffee, an inexperienced US Navy lawyer who has never managed a courtroom case, has to defend two Marines charged with the murder of another Marine called Santiago, at a base in Cuba. Kaffee just wants to plea-bargain rather than defend the two Marines properly. But he finds himself obliged to do so and, in the process, realises he likes trial work. Soon, however, he discovers that that it was Colonel Nathan Jessep, who's in charge of the men in the camp, who ordered that Santiago be disciplined for a misdemeanour. Kaffee forces Jessep to admit that he gave the order that led to Santiago's death. The two Marines are found guilty of conduct unbecoming and dishonourably discharged from the Marines. Kaffee has inspired truth over deceit and gains respect from all concerned.

THE SPEECH

Some speeches have the power and the fury to make the mind boggle. While we should be on the side of Kaffee, we recognise truths in what Jessep is saying because he inspires by his truths, his evident beliefs and his delivery:

“You can't handle the truth! Son, we live in a world that has walls. And those walls have to be guarded by men with guns. Who's gonna do it? You? … I have a greater responsibility than you can possibly fathom. You weep for Santiago and you curse the Marines. You have that luxury. You have the luxury of not knowing what I know: that Santiago's death, while tragic, probably saved lives. And my existence, while grotesque and incomprehensible to you, saves lives … You don't want the truth. Because deep down, in places you don't talk about at parties, you want me on that wall. You need me on that wall. We use words like honour, code, loyalty … we use these words as the backbone to a life spent defending something. You use 'em as a punchline. I have neither the time nor the inclination to explain myself to a man who rises and sleeps under the blanket of the very freedom I provide, then questions the manner in which I provide it! I'd rather you just said thank you and went on your way. Otherwise, I suggest you pick up a weapon and stand a post …”

FROM THE FILM

70 GLENGARRY GLEN ROSS

DIRECTED BY JAMES FOLEY (1992)

This excellent film is based on the Pulitzer Prize-winning David Mamet play of 1984 adapted by Mamet himself. It is about a number of real estate salesmen who become desperate over two days to sell their quotas, the non-achievement of which will result in their being fired.

THE STORY

All the sales executives in a New York real estate agency are finding their positions precarious. Blake, a sales motivator (Alec Baldwin), abuses them and teases them with sales incentives – first prize is a car and second – a set of steak knives. The third prize is the sack. Only the top two sellers will be allowed access to better leads, the others will be out. Long-term salesman Shelley Levene (Jack Lemmon) has an ill daughter and has been doing very badly in sales; he tries charm, bullying and bribery on agency manager John Williamson (Kevin Spacey) to get some of the super leads, but when Williamson finally agrees to sell some of these leads, Levene hasn't got the money.

Both Dave Moss (Ed Harris) and George Aaronow (Alan Arkin) complain about the owners of the agency. Moss wants to steal all the super leads and sell them to another agency, but Aaronow doesn't want to be involved. Ricky Roma (Al Pacino) is the agency's best salesman and tries to sell some real estate to a soft, insecure and gullible client, James Lingk (Jonathan Pryce).

The next day it's clear that all the good leads have been stolen. The police and Williamson interview each salesman one by one. Moss has a row with Roma and leaves, resenting the fact that he's under suspicion at all.

We find out that it was Levene and Moss behind the burglary. Levene tries to bribe Williamson into keeping quiet by promising a cut of future sales. Williamson scorns the offer. The ending shows a defeated Levene walking into the office where the police are waiting to interrogate him.

THE SPEECH

There's a powerful point in the story when super salesman Blake, who's been sent by the firm's owners to push up the agency's figures, gives the sale executives an ultimatum – deliver or you're out. Tough as it is, there's something here which generates a spark of possibility and it's that possibility that just might drive a salesman or woman forward. The alternative is nothing:

"Let's talk about something important! ... Put. That coffee. Down. Coffee's for closers only … The bad news is you've got, all of you got, just one week to regain your jobs, starting tonight … Oh, have I got your attention now? Good. 'Cause we're adding a little something to this month's sales contest. As you all know, first prize is a Cadillac Eldorado. Anybody want to see second prize? Second prize's a set of steak knives. Third prize is you're fired. You get the picture? You laughing now? A-B-C. A-always, B-be, C-closing. Always be closing! … You wanna work here? Close!! You think this is abuse? … Get mad! You sons of bitches! Get mad! … (He displays a large stack of red index cards tied together with string) These are the new leads. These are the Glengarry leads. And to you, they're gold and you don't get them. Why? Because to give them to you is just throwing them away. They're for closers. I'd wish you good luck but you wouldn't know what to do with it if you got it …"

FROM THE FILM

71 SCENT OF A WOMAN

DIRECTED BY MARTIN BREST (1992)

Adapted from the Italian novel, *Il Buio e il Miele* by Giovanni Arpino, it won Al Pacino an Oscar for Best Actor for his role as Lieutenant Colonel Frank Slade.

THE STORY

Charlie Simms is a seventeen year-old boy attending a top-notch American boarding school. Unlike most of the other boys, Charlie is not from an affluent background, but is there on a scholarship. One of his so-called friends, George Willis (Philip Seymour Hoffman), has a very nasty edge. George and his pals (but not Charlie) witness some damage to the school by a couple of classmates; the mean-spirited headmaster Trask (James Rebhorn) takes Charlie and George to task to find out the culprits' names, but the two boys will not tell, even though they know. Trask tells Charlie that unless he gets the names after the Thanksgiving holidays, he'll not recommend Charlie for Harvard.

Over the holidays, Charlie has a job looking after blind and retired Colonel Frank Slade for a few days. Slade takes Charlie on a series of adventures in New York, involving call girls and Ferraris. Charlie begins to understand the Colonel's own frustrations and hurt, and speaks about his school dilemma. The Colonel discovers Charlie to be honourable and decent.

After the holidays, Charlie still won't give Trask the names he wants so Trask decides to expel Charlie. When the whole school is assembled, Colonel Slade makes a brilliant and uplifting plea for Charlie's innocence; George and his cronies are shown up to be the unpleasant people they will undoubtedly remain.

THE SPEECH

There are some theatrical moments where we know a speech is so apposite and has such a ring of truth that it cannot be bettered. The speech given by blind Colonel Slade towards the end of this film is one such. Just as Trask is about to recommend Charlie's expulsion, the auditorium's doors bang open and there's the tapping of Slade's stick as he makes his way to the stage. Trask tells Slade that he's out of order.

“Outta order? I'll show you outta order! You don't know what outta order is, Mr. Trask! I'd show you but I'm too old; I'm too tired; I'm too fuckin' blind. If I were the man I was five years ago I'd take a flame-thrower to this place! Outta order. Who the hell you think you're talkin' to? I've been around, you know? There was a time I could see. And I have seen boys like these, younger than these, their arms torn out, their legs ripped off. But there isn't nothin' like the sight of an amputated spirit; there is no prosthetic for that. You think you're merely sendin' this splendid foot-soldier back home to Oregon with his tail between his legs, but I say you are executin' his soul! And why? Because he's not a Baird man! …

Mr. Trask: Stand down, Mr. Slade!

Slade: I'm not finished! … Makers of men, creators of leaders, be careful what kind of leaders you're producin' here. I don't know if Charlie's silence here today is right or wrong. I'm not a judge or jury. But I can tell you this: he won't sell anybody out to buy his future! And that, my friends, is called integrity! That's called courage! Now that's the stuff leaders should be made of …"

Colonel Slade finishes the speech with "… You hold this boy's future in your hands … It's a valuable future … Don't destroy it! Protect it. Embrace it. It's gonna make ya proud one day – I promise you."

And that speech, more than anything else, inspired me to write this book.

FROM THE FILM

72 UNFORGIVEN

DIRECTED BY CLINT EASTWOOD (1992)

The film, directed by and starring Eastwood, is a Western with a moral twist. It won four Academy Awards, including Best Director for Eastwood.

THE STORY

Big Whisky is an ordinary town with farmers and cowboys working more or less in harmony with one another. Sheriff Little Bill (Gene Hackman) is a frightening and unpopular law and order keeper. Some drunken, rogue cowboys cut the face of one of the local prostitutes and Little Bill insists that financial restitution is sufficient punishment. Disgusted with what passes for justice, the prostitutes put a bounty of $1,000 on the culprits. This attracts a very short-sighted youth who calls himself The Schofield Kid (Jaimz Woolvet) and ageing gunslinger William Munny (Clint Eastwood), now a struggling pig farmer and single father of two children. Munny calls on his old friend Ned (Morgan Freeman) to join him and seek their last fortune together.

This isn't a neat and tidy Western scenario with the good guy riding off into the sunset having vanquished all. There are no real good guys. There is literally no forgiveness. The violence and the retribution are effective and nasty.

THE SPEECH

The extract is the postscript text we see at the film's end, not a speech. However it inspires because we have seen a slice of American life as it most probably was in part. All the players are flawed as characters but in Eastwood's there is some humanity and gentleness which we hang on to because we want to and perhaps need to. The ending makes us wonder what has happened to the outlaw Munny, who has administered rough justice. Will's house is silhouetted on the horizon. Will walks towards the gravestone of his dead wife, Claudia, and stands still by it:

> “Some years later, Mrs. Ansonia Feathers made the arduous journey to Hodgeman County to visit the last resting place of her only daughter. William Munny had long since disappeared with the children ... some said to San Francisco where it was rumoured he prospered in dry goods. And there was nothing on the marker to explain to Mrs. Feathers why her only daughter had married a known thief and murderer, a man of notoriously vicious and intemperate disposition.”

When the text finishes its crawl, Will's figure has disappeared.

FROM THE FILM

73 SCHINDLER'S LIST

DIRECTED BY STEVEN SPIELBERG (1993)

This film, adapted from *Schindler's Ark,* by Thomas Keneally, published in 1982, won seven Academy Awards, including Best Director for Spielberg – his first. The book was based on interviews with Schindler survivors.

Apart from the beginning and end, and a little girl's coat picked out in red, the film is black and white. The story is presented almost as a documentary, although it is most definitely a drama. It is not in any way contrived and all the key characters are underplayed. The music, composed by John Williams, is powerful, moving, haunting and gaunt. This is an inspirational film on all levels, the ending in particular.

THE STORY

Oskar Schindler (Liam Neeson) was a real-life industrialist and opportunist before and during World War II in Nazi Sudetenland. Initially, he exploits the cheap labour provided by Jewish workers in an enamel and cookware factory, using flattery and bribes to win military contracts. He brings in Jewish accountant Itzhak Stern (Ben Kingsley), rescued from a death camp train, to help manage the workers and the factory. Schindler redirects a trainload of his male workers from Auschwitz to his hometown in Czechoslovakia. When the women's train is misrouted to Auschwitz in error, Schindler boldly strides into the death camp and bribes the commandant to ship them back out again.

In 1942, all of Krakow's Jews are assigned to the Plaszow Forced Labour Camp, overseen by Commandant Amon Goeth (Ralph Fiennes), a drunk who, for fun, takes pot shots at prisoners from his balcony. Schindler continues to use Polish Jews as cheap labour, but when he sees what happens to them on their return to the camp, begins to help them. His factory now makes ammunition and he can see that by employing more prisoners he can keep them reasonably safe. Soon Schindler demands more workers and starts bribing Nazi leaders to keep Jews on his employee lists.

At the very end of the film, with the war ended, Schindler's Jews walk off towards the horizon. The next shot fades from black and white into colour. We see what we believe are the same people, Schindler's list survivors, now returning along with their families, visiting Schindler's grave.

THE SPEECH

Inspiration doesn't appear in the form of hope very often in this film, but when it does, it soars and roars. In particular, when the end of the war is nigh, Oskar Schindler says farewell to his workers, announcing the unconditional surrender of Germany. His workers crowd around him to hear his modest words:

> "The unconditional surrender of Germany has just been announced ... Tomorrow you'll begin the process of looking for survivors of your families. In most cases ... you won't find them ... We've survived. Many of you have come up to me and thanked me. Thank yourselves ... I am a member of the Nazi Party. I'm a munitions manufacturer ... I am ... a criminal. At midnight, you'll be free and I'll be hunted ... [He now addresses the factory's SS guards] I know you have received orders ... to dispose of the population of this camp. Now would be the time to do it. Here they are; they're all here. This is your opportunity. Or, you could leave, and return to your families as men instead of murderers."
> [The guards gradually exit]

Later, Schindler has to leave and bids farewell to his close colleague, Stern. Schindler breaks down.

"Schindler: I could have got more out. I could have got more. I don't know. If I'd just ... I could have got more.

Stern: Oskar, there are eleven hundred people who are alive because of you. Look at them.

Schindler: If I'd made more money ... I threw away so much money. You have no idea. If I'd just ...

Stern: There will be generations because of what you did.

Schindler: I didn't do enough!

Stern: You did so much …

Schindler: I could have got one more person ... and I didn't! And I ... I didn't!”

FROM THE FILM

74 MRS. DOUBTFIRE

DIRECTED BY CHRIS COLUMBUS (1993)

In this film, adored by adults and children alike, we delight in the supreme talent that Robin Williams brings to the title role. Deservedly, the film won an Academy Award for makeup.

THE STORY

Daniel Hilliard (Robin Williams) is an actor struggling to find roles. He suddenly finds himself divorced because his wife, Miranda (Sally Fields), is fed up with his childishness and feels they have nothing in common anymore. Miranda gets custody of the three children. Daniel adores his children and the thought of not seeing them for more than once a week is agony to him. To solve this problem, he disguises himself as a tough but adorable Scottish nanny to get hired by his estranged wife and be closer to the children. His children and Miranda have no idea that Daniel is Mrs. Doubtfire. In the process of being her and being with the children more, Daniel gets to understand how to be a better parent.

Johnathan Lundy (Robert Prosky), the CEO of the TV station where Daniel works as a clerk, notices Daniel playing with some toys on the set of a particularly boring children's programme. He arranges to meet Daniel for dinner to discuss ideas – at the same restaurant Miranda and family, along with new boyfriend Stu (Pierce Brosnan), are having a birthday dinner for Miranda. Daniel spends most of the evening swapping from men's clothes to women's. Gradually he gets quite drunk, puts pepper on Stu's shrimp, then helps Stu when he chokes. In the process, he blows his cover.

Miranda now has full custody of the children but she and the children are unhappy without Mrs. Doubtfire. Daniel, meanwhile is becoming very successful as Mrs. Doubtfire, on a new TV programme for kids. Impressed by Daniel's success, Miranda asks him to come back as himself – to take care of the children after school. She sorts out the court ruling. We assume (or hope) that eventually all will be well again.

THE SPEECH

Towards the end of the film, Daniel, dressed as Mrs. Doubtfire, on his new, successful TV programme, gives out regular advice to children who write in. Miranda sees and hears Daniel reading out one letter from a little girl. It inspires the audience in the film and also the film's audience (us):

"Katie: Dear Mrs. Doubtfire, two months ago my mom and dad decided to separate … My brother Andrew says that we aren't to be a family anymore. Is this true? Did I lose my family? Is there anything I can do to get my parents back together? Sincerely, Katie McCormick.

Mrs. Doubtfire: Oh my dear Katie. You know some parents, when they're angry, they get along much better when they don't live together. They don't fight all the time and they can become better people and much better mummies and daddies for you. And sometimes they get back together. And sometimes they don't dear. And if they don't, don't blame yourself. Just because they don't love each other anymore, doesn't mean that they don't love you … But if there's love, dear ... those are the ties that bind, and you'll have a family in your heart, forever. All my love to you poppet, you're going to be alright ... bye bye."

FROM THE FILM

75 FOUR WEDDINGS AND A FUNERAL

DIRECTED BY MIKE NEWELL (1994)

This very British romantic comedy, starring Hugh Grant, has enormous charm, grace and humour.

THE STORY

Charles (Hugh Grant), a hesitant, floppy-haired, pleasant and good-hearted Englishman, is always late, not least for weddings. He and his close group of friends are all seeking romance apart from the gay couple Gareth (Simon Callow) and Matthew (John Hannah), who have it already. At the wedding of friends, Angus (Timothy Walker) and Laura (Sarah Crowe), best man Charles meets and falls head over heels for Carrie (Andie MacDowell). The feeling is mutual, but Charles doesn't follow up. They meet up again at three more weddings and Gareth's funeral. Charles and Carrie feel strongly about each other but, for one reason or another, they don't end up as a couple. Carrie seems unattainable. Charles believes that perhaps he should settle down with one of his ex-girlfriends. Carrie marries wealthy Sir Hamish Banks (Corin Redgrave) and Charles feels almost obliged to marry Henrietta (Anna Chancellor), but Carrie turns up again and Charles has third and fourth thoughts.

THE SPEECH

The recitation of Funeral Blues, beginning with "Stop all the clocks ..." by W.H. Auden, is one of the film's most memorable and inspirational moments. Matthew gives a poignant reading of the poem at the funeral of his partner, Gareth. That the poem is actually about a lover who has walked out on Auden, rather than the death of a true love, isn't really the point. The point is that the poem works for the moment and its words are beautifully declaimed. They put a context to our thinking.

FROM THE FILM

76 THE SHAWSHANK REDEMPTION

DIRECTED BY FRANK DARABONT (1994)

This film is hugely powerful as a drama about American prison life and a man's management of his time in prison. It is adapted from a Stephen King story called *Rita Hayworth and the Shawshank Redemption* (1982) and is a roller-coaster of a movie with emotional highs and lows. The storytelling is great with, once again, good coming out of hardship.

THE STORY

Andy (Tim Robbins) is wrongly imprisoned for murdering his wife. He's sent to Shawshank prison for a double life sentence. There he makes friends with Red (Morgan Freeman), who manages to smuggle a rock hammer and a poster of Rita Hayworth for Andy from the outside world. Andy is good with financial advice and is soon besieged by requests to help guards from this and other prisons. The warden (Bob Gunton) gets Andy to manage some illegal financial dealings and money laundering. As a result of this newfound trust, Andy builds up the prison library.

A newcomer named Tommy (Gil Bellows) tells Andy that in another prison he talked to an inmate Ernie (Joseph Ragno), who said that it was he who killed Andy's wife and that Andy was framed. When Andy tells the warden, the warden isn't interested as he wants to keep Andy in jail. Instead he has Tommy shot.

Andy disappears one day. The guards find a hole in his cell wall dug with the geology hammer and hidden by the Hayworth poster. The hole had taken Andy twenty years to dig. And he has used the warden's scams to line his own pockets to the tune of twenty years' worth of salary. The police find out about the warden's dishonesty and he commits suicide. Red gets out of prison on parole (after forty years), finds money left by Andy, and the two reunite in Mexico.

THE SPEECH

There are several moments where hope seems to be bleak or lost, where there can be seemingly no good to come out of the story's blackness or inability to achieve, where the future must stretch out before someone falsely imprisoned in a way that few of us can ever imagine. Where there is hope in the film, we delight in the moment only often to have that moment dashed. Inspiration rises at the film's end, when we applaud the fact that the warden has not won on any count and where the prison hasn't held Andy. We applaud the fact that, at long last, Red has his parole and we applaud the fact that these two essentially decent, good people are free. We are inspired by the fact all will be well now.

The inspiration that frames the terrible scenarios within the prison and its system is borne out in a couple of notes actually, not speeches. Here is a note Andy left for Red:

> “There’s a big hayfield up near Buxton ... one in particular. It’s got a long rock wall, a big oak tree at the north end. It’s like something out of a Robert Frost poem. It’s where I asked my wife to marry me. We went there for a picnic and made love under that oak and I asked and she said yes. Promise me, Red. If you ever get out, find that spot. In the base of that wall, you’ll find a rock that has no earthly business in a Maine hayfield. A piece of black, volcanic glass. There’s something buried under it I want you to have.”

And when Red finds the small box, there’s another note:

> “Dear Red, if you’re reading this, you’ve gotten out. And if you’ve come this far, maybe you’re willing to come a little further. You remember the name of the town, don’t you? I could use a good man to help me get my project on wheels. I’ll keep an eye out for you and the chessboard ready. Remember, Red. Hope is a good thing – maybe the best of things and no good thing ever dies. I will be hoping that this letter finds you and finds you well. Your friend, Andy.”

FROM THE FILM

77 FORREST GUMP

DIRECTED BY ROBERT ZEMECKIS (1994)

Sometimes a film comes along that is more or less totally inspirational on a wide variety of levels. *Forrest Gump* is one such. The film, starring Tom

Hanks, is based on a Winston Groom novel of the same name published in 1986. It won the Academy Award for Best Director, Best Picture and Best Actor. It's a film from which people quote constantly. That's an inspirational accolade in itself.

THE STORY

Forrest Gump (Tom Hanks) is simple and always means well. His childhood is tough but he gets through it supported by his best friend Jenny (Robin Wright Penn) and his mother (Sally Field) who teaches him life's basic rules. As he grows up, he has a vast number of adventures – including fighting in Vietnam, winning medals, beating the Chinese national team at table tennis, building a huge shrimp business, running across the whole of the US, becoming a football sensation, giving money away, teaching Elvis to dance, meeting presidents (Kennedy, Johnson, Nixon) and investing in Apple at the very start. He turns up (by accident) at important historical moments and always thinks of Jenny whom he loves, but Jenny has made a mess of her life. At the film's end, he wins Jenny, but she dies leaving him with a son, also called Forrest.

THE SPEECH

There are many wonderful one liners that create superb inspiration in context – for example, when Forrest proudly and famously declares: "My momma always said, 'Life was like a box of chocolates. You never know what you're gonna get.'" But there is a moment towards the end, when we hear Forrest's voiceover as we see the tree under which Jenny is buried. It is an inspiring and emotional piece that sums up Forrest's naivety, kindness and essential goodness.

"You died on a Saturday morning. And I had you placed here under our tree ... Little Forrest, he's doing just fine ... I make sure he combs his hair and brushes his teeth every day. Teaching him how to play ping-pong. He's really good ... He's so smart, Jenny. You'd be so proud of him. I am. He, uh, wrote a letter, and he says I can't read it ... so I'll just leave it here for you … I don't know if we each have a destiny, or if we're all just floating around accidental-like on a breeze, but I, I think maybe it's both … I miss you, Jenny. If there's anything you need, I won't be far away.”

FROM THE FILM

78 PULP FICTION

DIRECTED BY QUENTIN TARANTINO (1994)

This is a violent film with black comedic moments. It won an Oscar for Best Original Screenplay and has achieved cult status since. The film's language is delicious and there are entertaining bits of dialogue that charm and give perspectives of life. This is very different fare from the normal adventure or crime movie. The film's dialogue is probably the most quoted. It quickly came to be regarded as one of the most significant films of the decade.

THE STORY

There are several story strands which, from time to time, meet each other. The three core ones involve firstly Vincent Vega (John Travolta), a hit man and thug, the second, Butch Coolidge (Bruce Willis) and the third, another hit man and partner to Vincent, Jules Winnfield (Samuel L. Jackson).

The film begins with a hold-up in a restaurant by Pumpkin (Tim Roth) and Honey Bunny (Amanda Plummer). Vincent and Jules are on their way to dispose of Brett (Frank Whaley), a smaller thug, who has done something against their boss, Marsellus Wallace (Ving Rhames). We find out much later that Pumpkin and Honey are allowed by Vincent and Jules to leave the restaurant with stolen money.

Meanwhile prizefighter Butch accepts a lot of money from Marsellus to lose a forthcoming fight and Vincent has been tasked to look after Marsellus' girlfriend, Mia Wallace (Uma Thurman), while he is away. Vincent and Mia win a dance competition after which they go back to her home where she finds Vincent's supply of cocaine in his coat pocket. She overdoses. With help, Vincent revives Mia.

We next see Butch as a boy and the arrival of Captain Koons (Christopher Walken) who was in Vietnam and has come to bring a watch passed to him by Butch's father who died in a POW camp. The adult Butch awakes from the daydream and is about to fight the fight he's been paid to lose. But he doesn't lose and instead accidentally kills the other fighter, which greatly upsets Marsellus. Lying low, he discovers he's left his father's watch at home so he goes home to get it. At his apartment he comes face to face with Vincent, whom he kills. In the ensuing confusion, Butch and Marsellus end up in a pawn shop and the owner ties them up. The shop owner's accomplice rapes Marsellus and Butch frees himself to kill the shopkeeper. Marsellus manages to shoot the rapist and tells Butch they're now quits.

We now come back to Vincent and Jules just after they've disposed of Brett. Another man shoots at them but is killed instead. Jules wants to retire as a hitman thinking that what he's just experienced is a sign from God. They have one of Brett's associates in the car whom they shoot by accident. They seek help from someone known as The Wolf (Harvey Keitel) to get the car cleaned, the body disposed of and everything made good. Then they go for breakfast at the diner where the hold-up at the film's start is taking place.

THE SPEECH

Of several superb moments in this film, one in particular deserves the epithet inspirational. It's when Captain Koons brings young Butch his father's watch. It's an important moment in the film because it's the reason that Butch goes back to collect the watch when that's clearly a suicidal move. Butch also gets to know something special and inspirational about his father:

“Hello, little man … I was a good friend of your dad's. We were in that Hanoi pit of hell together for over five years … [Holds up watch] This watch I got here was first purchased by your great-grandfather during the First World War. It was bought in a little general store in Knoxville, Tennessee … Then when he had done his duty, he went home to your great-grandmother, took the watch and put it in an old coffee can. And in that can it stayed 'til your granddad, Dane Coolidge, was called upon by his country to go overseas and fight the Germans once again ... Your great-grandfather gave this watch to your granddad for good luck. Unfortunately, Dane's luck wasn't as good as his old man's ... your granddad asked a gunner on an Air Force transport ... to deliver to his infant son, who he had never seen in the flesh, his gold watch. Three days later, your granddad was dead ... This watch was on your Daddy's wrist when he was shot down over Hanoi. He was captured and put in a Vietnamese prison camp ... The way your Dad looked at it, this watch was your birthright ... So he hid it in the one place he knew he could hide something. His ass. Five long years, he wore this watch up his ass. Then he died of dysentery, he gave me the watch. I hid this uncomfortable hunk of metal up my ass for two years. Then, after seven years, I was sent home to my family. And now, little man, I give the watch to you."

FROM THE FILM

79 RICHARD III

DIRECTED BY RICHARD LONCRAINE (1995)

Richard III is one of the most memorable of Shakespeare's characters. The play, about the deformed villain who's loathed and filled with self-loathing, was written around 1591. The film of the play starred Ian McKellan in the title role.

This version of the play is set in a fascist state in the 1930s. It won two Academy Awards.

THE STORY

After years of civil war between the Royal Houses of York and Lancaster, the Yorkist Edward IV is undisputed king. Richard of Gloucester, the king's younger brother, is jealous and wants the English throne; he murders his way to it, including getting rid of their brother Clarence and allowing the blame to fall on the king. Richard engineers the death of Henry VI's son and then woos and marries his widow Anne. After the death of Edward, Richard kills the court noblemen loyal to King Edward's heirs and has the boys' powerful kinsmen on their mother's (Queen Elizabeth) side executed. Richard, with support from his king-maker, Lord Buckingham, plans to get himself crowned king. He imprisons the young princes in the Tower and has them murdered. Buckingham, who has refused to be party to these murders, escapes Richard and joins Henry Tudor, Earl of Richmond, a descendant of the Lancastrian family and who is waiting in France for his chance to move against Richard.

To consolidate his power, Richard has his wife Anne murdered, so he is free to marry young Elizabeth, daughter of the former Queen Elizabeth and the dead Edward IV. Though young Elizabeth is his niece, the alliance would secure his claim to the throne. But Elizabeth has secretly been promised to the Earl of Richmond by her mother. Richard's plans now start to unravel.

Richmond finally invades England from France. The night before the battle, Richard has a terrible dream in which the ghosts of all the people he has murdered appear and curse him, telling him he will die the next day. In the battle at Bosworth Field, Richard is indeed killed and Richmond is crowned King Henry VII. As the new king is betrothed to young Elizabeth, there's promise of a new era of peace.

THE SPEECH

There is little at the start of the film/play that one might imagine is inspired speech. However, at the very beginning we *are* inspired when we first hear of what Richard is and what he has become. We are not yet fully tainted with his record of death or his scheming, but we are impressed by the strength of his words and how they are delivered. We might even feel a little sorry for him. It's a powerful speech and superb rhetoric.

The film opens with the murder of reigning King Henry VI (Edward Jewesbury) by the treacherous Duke of Gloucester (Ian McKellen) – soon to be Richard III – who then delivers the victory speech into a microphone before his entire family and guests at a royal ball:

"Now is the winter of our discontent
Made glorious summer by this sun of York;
And all the clouds that lour'd upon our house
In the deep bosom of the ocean buried.
Now are our brows bound with victorious wreaths;
Our bruised arms hung up for monuments;
Our stern alarums changed to merry meetings,
Our dreadful marches to delightful measures …"

He finishes the monologue muttering as he stands at a urinal and turns to the camera to deliver this line and now we know that he's a villain:

"I am determined to prove a villain.
And hate the idle pleasures of these days.
Plots have I laid to set my brothers Clarence and King Edward
In deadly hate the one against the other."

If you're a Shakespeare purist, this film is not for you. The original text has been cut and shaped to suit this production. The quote above is a case in point where the "now is the winter of our discontent" speech gets chopped more or less in half. McKellen inspires us with the interpretation, not in making evil good, but in making language work as an inspirational driver.

FROM THE FILM

80 TRAINSPOTTING

DIRECTED BY DANNY BOYLE (1996)

This film is an adaptation of the 1993 novel of the same name by Irvine Walsh and is narrated by Renton (Ewan McGregor). It's a film that explores poverty and squalor and one which lays bare the open sore lives of drug addicts in Edinburgh and what they will do to get their next fix.

THE STORY

A group of down-at-heel young men escape the day-to-day grind of modern life by taking heroin and/or copious amounts of alcohol. Renton wants to stop taking heroin, but can't. He convinces himself that there are good reasons why he shouldn't give up. He doesn't want to face daily reality. Sick Boy (Jonny Lee Miller) uses his heroin habit as an excuse to steal. He has no morals and relates everything to the life of Sean Connery although he knows nothing about Sean Connery. Begbie (Robert Carlyle) is violent and a psychopath. He drinks too much and is invariably out of control. Spud (Ewan Bremner) ensures that he never gets a job by taking speed before any interview. Tommy (Kevin McKidd) never took any drugs and did nothing illegal but that all changes when he's dumped by his girlfriend.

Through each character we see a different side of Renton's own personality. Renton promises his parents and a judge that he will give up heroin, but instead takes a very strong dose. After a spell in hospital, his parents lock him in his room and his withdrawal is a terrifying, living nightmare. He does become clean and also tests negative for HIV. Tommy has tested positive for HIV and is living in absolute squalor.

Renton moves to London and starts a job in an estate agency. He likes the life in London. When Begbie and Sick Boy show up at his flat, Renton feels he can't send them away. They steal from him and create havoc so he puts them in a property he's trying to sell. They all return to Scotland because Tommy has died. In Edinburgh they meet Spud who has just been released from prison. They become involved in a deal to sell an amount of heroin in London for a huge profit. Renton steals most of the money and lives the stable life he has always wanted.

THE SPEECH

In the opening shots, we see two men running fast along a street. The soundtrack is Iggy Pop's song, *Lust for Life*. Over the beat of the music we hear a young Scottish voiceover on what life should be. While the words are snarled at us, they will brook no denial; we are inspired. What follows is Renton's shopping list of what we should believe:

"Choose life. Choose a job. Choose a career. Choose a family. Choose a fucking big television. Choose washing machines, cars, compact disc players and electrical tin openers. Choose good health, low cholesterol and dental insurance … Choose rottin' away at the end of it all, pissing your last in a miserable home … Choose a future. Choose life ... But why would I want to do a thing like that? I chose not to choose life. I chose somethin' else. And the reasons? There are no reasons. Who needs reasons when you've got heroin? So why did I do it? … The truth is that … I'm going to change. This is the last of that sort of thing, and I'm cleanin' up … and choosin' life … I'm going to be just like you: the job, the family, the fucking big television ..."

FROM THE PLAY

81 MY BOY JACK

WRITTEN BY DAVID HAIG (1997)

This three-act play tells the story of poet Rudyard Kipling's relationship with his son, John (Jack). The title of the play is also the title of the 1916 poem Kipling wrote after the huge Battle of Jutland, the biggest sea battle of World War I.

In the play, Kipling forces his son to enlist and go off to France and fight despite the boy's poor eyesight and his ambivalence about the army. Jack dies in the Battle of Loos in 1915. The play has won many critical plaudits and English actor David Haig has also played the lead in the TV adaptation (2007). The play and poem of the same name are haunting, more so when we know that Kipling's most famous poem, *If*, had been written for his son and that Jack died just six weeks after his eighteenth birthday. It is said that Kipling blamed himself for his son's death.

THE STORY

Act one shows seventeen year-old Jack trying on a pair of spectacles. His eyesight is poor and he fails his eye test. His father, Rudyard Kipling, is a firm, direct and controlling figure. Jack feels bullied by his father and suffocated by his father's fame. He confides to his sister Elsie that he wants to join the army to escape. Elsie is cross because she fears for his life and she's not totally convinced that Jack really wants to join up. Later, Kipling tells Jack he'll get the young man into the army somehow. Jack joins the army and leads men into battle.

Act two sees the Kipling family receiving news that Jack is reported missing. Kipling is wracked by guilt for making Jack join the war. Elsie tells the family that it wasn't patriotism that made Jack join up.

Act three shows Elsie about to marry and the Kipling family beginning to live again. It is six years after the war. Rudyard Kipling has been talking to army witnesses from Jack's regiment in the interim. One reports that Jack had been leading a charge and continued when others stopped or fell away. We learn that Jack was killed by machine gun fire. We move forward another nine years and there are mutterings about another war. Kipling agonises over his son's death. The play ends with Kipling's poem, *My Boy Jack.*

THE SPEECH

The speech is the poem. It begins:

> “Have you news of my boy Jack?”

Do read it all. It's simple, powerful and heart-wrenching in its reading. Kipling was to write a regimental history of the Irish Guards, Jack's regiment, considered to be one of the finest ever histories written and which contains a heartbreakingly brief description of his own son's death. Kipling was never able to write directly about his loss. The poem, *My Boy Jack,* is about a sailor, but is a thinly disguised poem about regret and mourning.

FROM THE FILM

82 GOOD WILL HUNTING

DIRECTED BY GUS VAN SANT (1997)

This film was written by and stars Matt Damon and Ben Affleck, supported on screen by Robin Williams. Damon plays Will Hunting – a prodigy mathematician who sweeps floors at Massachusetts Institute of Technology (MIT). Affleck and Damon won an Academy Award for Best Original Screenplay; Robin Williams won an Academy Award for Best Supporting Actor.

THE STORY

Will Hunting was abused as a child and has been in and out of trouble ever since, often with his best friend, Chuckie (Ben Affleck). He's brilliant at mathematics – evidenced by his solution to a problem left on an MIT blackboard. Professor Lambeau (Stellan Skarsgard), who left the problem, is amazed that a janitor solved it. Will is in trouble with the police over some misdemeanour and the professor offers him a way out – but only if he visits a therapist and attends weekly mathematics lessons. The professor asks a therapist friend, Sean Maguire (Robin Williams), to help Will manage his genius; in the process, Will and Sean both manage their pasts.

Sean has been unable to deal with his wife's premature death from cancer two years before. The relationship between Will and Sean grows into friendship. Professor Lambeau has high expectations of Will, but Sean doesn't believe that Will should be pushed so hard. Meanwhile Will meets medical student Skylar (Minnie Driver), who wants Will to move with her to the West Coast. Will declines and pushes both Skylar and Lambeau away. Sean is aware that Will always anticipates failure in his relationships so he allows them to fizzle out or deliberately moves away from them.

Will tells Chuckie that he wants to be a blue collar worker forever. Chuckie is furious. He says that his greatest wish is to knock on Will's door one morning and find he isn't there. Will makes up his mind to drive his own life. Sean decides to travel the world.

Will receives a car for his birthday, given to him by Chuckie and his friends. When Chuckie knocks on Will's door and there's no reply, Chuckie knows that his friend has gone to seek his potential.

THE SPEECH

There's a marvellous moment of which we're envious, when Will gets into an argument with an arrogant, loud and rude student at a Harvard bar who affects to know a great deal about economics. This is inspired and it's wonderful to behold because you want to shout "yippee!" and wish fervently that you could do something similar:

"Of course that's your contention. You're a first year grad student. You just got finished readin' some Marxian historian – Pete Garrison probably. You're gonna be convinced of that 'til next month when you get to James Lemon and then you're gonna be talkin' about how the economies of Virginia and Pennsylvania were entrepreneurial and capitalist way back in 1740. That's gonna last until next year – you're gonna be in here regurgitating Gordon Wood, talkin' about, you know, the Pre-Revolutionary utopia and the capital-forming effects of military mobilization ... You got that from Vickers, 'Work in Essex County', page 98, right? Yeah, I read that too. Were you gonna plagiarize the whole thing for us? .... You come into a bar. You read some obscure passage and then pretend ... you pawn it off as your own idea just to impress some girls and embarrass my friend? ..."

FROM THE FILM

83 LIFE IS BEAUTIFUL

DIRECTED BY ROBERTO BENIGNI (1997)

This Italian film (*La Vita è Bella*), starring Benigni, won three Oscars, including Best Actor for Benigni, who also co-wrote the story with Vincenzo Cerami. That they have created an inspirational film about Nazism, fascism, prejudice and concentration camp life with seriousness, humour, pathos and wit is quite extraordinary. If there's one film alone in this collection of inspirational moments, this one rises to the very top.

THE STORY

Guido Orefice (Roberto Benigni) is a cheerful, engaging Jewish man with a huge zest for life and who falls in love with Dora (Nicoletta Braschi) – who is not Jewish – in 1930s' Italy. They marry and have a son, Giosue (Joshua). For a time, their lives are idyllic.

War begins and Guido and his son are arrested and taken to a concentration camp. Dora insists on going too. To protect his little boy, Guido pretends that the family is just on holiday and makes sure his son sees the whole experience as a game. He tells Joshua they have to win one thousand points to win a real tank to go home.

As times in the camp get worse, Guido is separated from Dora, but he still tries to protect Joshua from the wretched truth. Joshua begins to be suspicious of the games and wonders if he will see a tank. The end of the film is so heart-wrenching and appalling that it's hard to watch. The Germans know that the Americans are on the way and they begin to shoot camp prisoners and then run off. Guido hides Joshua in a box from which the boy can see his father, still joking. Guido is approached by a camp soldier, taken behind a wall and shot dead. Joshua doesn't understand. He gets out of the box to see an American tank rolling towards him and belives that he has won the game. Mother and son are reunited.

THE SPEECH

The themes of inspiration and survival run brightly throughout the film. With Joshua we have hope. Here are a couple of scenes. The first piece is when anti-Semitism begins to spread in Italy and eventually hits home:

“Joshua: 'No Jews or Dogs Allowed.' Why do all the shops say, 'No Jews Allowed'?

Guido: Oh, that. 'Not Allowed' signs are the latest trend! The other day, I was in a shop with my friend the kangaroo, but their sign said, 'No

Kangaroos Allowed' and I said to my friend, "Well, what can I do? They don't allow kangaroos."

Joshua: Why doesn't our shop have a 'Not Allowed' sign?

Guido: Well, tomorrow, we'll put one up. We won't let in anything we don't like. What don't you like?

Joshua: Spiders.

Guido: Good. I don't like Visigoths. Tomorrow, we'll get the sign: 'No Spiders or Visigoths Allowed'."

And here is a small piece of dialogue when Guido and his small son board the train on its way to a concentration camp. The sight is terrifying for Guido and frightening for Joshua:

"Guido: You've never ridden on a train, have you? They're fantastic! Everybody stands up, close together and there are no seats!

Joshua: There aren't any seats?

Guido: Seats? On a train? It's obvious you've never ridden one before! No, everybody's packed in, standing up. Look at this line to get on! Hey, we've got tickets, save room for us!"

And, once off the train:

"Joshua: I didn't like the train.

Guido: Me, neither. We'll take the bus back, okay? [to the Nazi guards who doesn't understand Italian] Did you hear that? We're taking the bus back!"

At the end of the film, Joshua is reunited with his mother. Having seen the American tank, he believes he's won the game set up by Guido.

"Joshua: We won!

Dora: Yes, we won! It's true.

Joshua: We got a thousand points and we won the game! Daddy and me came in first and now we won the real tank! We won! We won!"

FROM THE FILM
84 ANTZ

DIRECTED BY ERIC DARNELL AND TIM JOHNSON (1998)

This animated movie, the first delivered by DreamWorks, featured the voices of Woody Allen, Sylvester Stallone, Sharon Stone, Gene Hackman, Dan Ackroyd and Christopher Walken. It is computer-generated and the second to be completed this way, *Toy Story* being the first.

THE STORY

Z4195 (Woody Allen) is a worker ant very fed up with the fact that millions of worker ants are all the same. There's no individuality. He meets the beautiful Princess Bala (Sharon Stone) who's a bit fed up because she's bored. Z sees her in a bar and dances with her without knowing who she is, becomes smitten and tries to see her again. He swaps roles with soldier ant Weaver (Sylvester Stallone) to see the princess at a parade, during which he makes friends with Barbatus (Danny Glover). Z then realises with horror that he's actually marching into battle. As the only survivor of the slaughter, Z returns home a war hero. He comes across General Mandible (Gene Hackman), Bala's fiance, who plans to divide the ant society into a superior, stronger race of soldier ants led by him and an inferior, disposable race made up of the workers (including Z). Bala and Z escape to find Insectopia, an overflowing rubbish bin – brilliant for ants.

Mandible sends his aide, Colonel Cutter (Christopher Walken), to Insectopia to get the Princess back and kill Z. When he takes Bala back to the colony, Z mounts a rescue bid, helped by a wasp called Chip (Dan Ackroyd). Z learns about Mandible's plot to drown the colony's queen ant along with all the workers. The day is saved by the ants all working together as a huge team. Bala and Z are married.

THE SPEECH

At the end of the film, Z rounds up everything neatly. Here to underline the feel-good factor is some inspirational ant philosophy:

"So there you have it. Your average 'boy-meets-girl, boy-likes-girl, boy-changes-underlying-social-order' story. So, what else can I tell you? We rebuilt the colony – it's even better than before, you know, 'cause now it has a very large indoor swimming pool. Bala and I, incidentally, are thinking of starting a family, you know, just a few kids, maybe a million or two to begin with. And I'm workin' with a new therapist, you know, terrific, absolutely terrific. He's been putting me in touch with my inner maggot, which is really helping me. And, you know, I finally feel like I've found my place, and you know what? It's right back where I started. But the difference is, this time I chose it."

Pure Woody Allen – vintage, heart-warming, lifting and invigorating stuff.

FROM THE FILM

85 SHAKESPEARE IN LOVE

DIRECTED BY JOHN MADDEN (1998)

This film is a romantic comedy, with an excellent script, based on a very good fun plot concerning William Shakespeare as he struggles to find his theatrical feet in 16th century London. The film won seven Academy Awards, including Best Picture and Best Actress (Gwyneth Paltrow).

THE STORY

William Shakespeare (Joseph Fiennes) is a struggling playwright/actor in London. He is married but separated. A wealthy beauty, Viola de Lesseps (Gweneth Paltrow), wants to tread the boards, but then women weren't allowed to act. She's an admirer of Shakespeare's, but is about to be married to the rather dull, cold and broke Lord Wessex (Colin Firth). Viola dresses as a young man and auditions successfully for the part of Romeo. Shakespeare discovers Viola's identity and they begin a passionate and secret affair. Some of their conversations "become" famous lines in the play.

Shakespeare struggles to stage Romeo and Juliet. Eventually Richard

Burbage (Martin Clunes) offers his own theatre and Shakespeare and Viola play opposite each other, he as Romeo and she as Juliet. Audiences are so touched by the inspiration and passion of the two lovers that the play is an enormous hit.

But Viola and Shakespeare must part, he to write *Twelfth Night* and she to sail to Virginia.

THE SPEECH

The story ebbs and flows with japes and jests and we enjoy the journey. Its language and wit are rich:

> “Shakespeare: I have a new play.
> Christopher Marlowe: What's it called?
> Shakespeare: Romeo and Ethel the Pirate's Daughter.
> Christopher Marlow: What is the story?
> Shakespeare: Well, there's this pirate... In truth I have not written a word.”

There's also inspiration in the love of life and the love of love. This from Viola to her nurse played by Imelda Staunton:

> “I will have poetry in my life. And adventure. And love. Love above all. No ... not the artful postures of love, not playful and poetical games of love for the amusement of an evening, but love that ... overthrows life. Unbiddable, ungovernable – like a riot in the heart, and nothing to be done, come ruin or rapture. Love – like there has never been in a play.”

AN OVERVIEW OF CHAPTER SEVEN

Throughout history, wisdom has been conveyed through fairy tales. The tale of *Edward Scissorhands* is no exception. While mercilessly exposing what people are generally like and the true nature of human beings, this tragic and satirical story is painful and yet full of hope. And maybe that's the prime reason for art – to give us hope.

Joe Versus the Volcano also has oodles of charm, humour and hope, but it's a different fairytale. The real story here is about coming to terms with oneself and finding the spark that many of us find and sometimes lose. It's also about discovering (our) humanity and what that means. In *Glengarry Glen Ross*, Jack Lemmon (Shelley) looks shocked, askance, dazed and desperate all in one when Alec Baldwin (Blake) yells, "Put that coffee down! Coffee's for closers." The look sums up a major theme of the play/film. As does the snappy Blake comment, "You see this watch? This watch costs more than your car". Mamet's character-driven screenplay delves into the place of our souls and psyches where desperation exists. It lurks as a stark reality to a lesser or greater degree in all of us.

Acidic realism is something that strikes a chord throughout *Schindler's List*. As the Jews in Kraków are forced into the ghetto, a little girl on the street repeatedly cries out, "Good-bye, Jews". The girl did not inherently have this hatred built into her psyche – she learned it. This is the film's core message, that people followed the evil leadership of a few who believed that they were doing right or because they had an evil streak allowed to run free. Understanding good versus evil is something that many stories explore and over which many people argue. In *The Shawshank Redemption* we have a poignant film with a powerful message of brutality and hope and the redemption we all seek at some point. Here, once again, is a mirror on us all.

Brutal is also a descriptor of Shakespeare's protagonist in *Richard III*. This Richard transforms his murderous whims into policy. McKellen makes Richard's grandiose ego mesmerising. He confides in us with such confidence that we almost find ourselves beginning to believe (quite comfortably) in his allure as a leader. Perhaps that's because the 1930s period lends itself to decadent royalty strutting the European stage, having a last dance, a last bit of fun before the Nazi beast pounces.

It can be said that *Life is Beautiful* has less to do with the Holocaust and more to do with the beautiful relationship between a father and his son. The

Holocaust provides the ultimate context and backdrop. Here is a rare story where tears of laughter and sadness intertwine. This is a film about human spirit above all else. Every convention known to Shakespeare in his time has been artfully adopted to give *Shakespeare in Love* its warmth and pathos. In this film, as in Shakespeare's plays, words matter, performance matters, wit and cleverness matter and, ultimately, theatre can give meaning to anyone's life. And that matters.

Chapter Eight

THE NOUGHTIES

Sam: "... By rights we shouldn't even be here. But we are. It's like in the great stories, Mr. Frodo. The ones that really mattered. Full of darkness and danger, they were. And sometimes you didn't want to know the end. Because how could the end be happy? How could the world go back to the way it was when so much bad had happened? But in the end, it's only a passing thing, this shadow. Even darkness must pass. A new day will come. And when the sun shines it will shine out the clearer. Those were the stories that stayed with you. That meant something, even if you were too small to understand why. But I think, Mr. Frodo, I do understand. I know now. Folk in those stories had lots of chances of turning back, only they didn't. They kept going. Because they were holding on to something." Sean Astin as Sam in *The Lord of the Rings: The Two Towers* (2002)

Thug: "What you lookin' at old man?"
Walt Kowalski: "Ever notice how you come across somebody once in a while you shouldn't have messed with? That's me." Clint Eastwood as Walt in *Gran Torino* (2008)

One of the markers of the decade must be the 2001 9/11 attacks in the US. That led to the war on terrorism and then the war in Afghanistan. A coalition led by the US invaded Iraq and ended Saddam Hussein's rule. Al-Qaeda was responsible for many terrorist attacks throughout the decade. There were and are nuclear threats posed by North Korea and Iran. The EU grew, taking under its wing a number of Eastern European countries. In the Middle East, Israel and Hezbollah were in conflict, as were Hamas and Israel.

The decade was marked by huge natural disasters: the 2004 tsunami, stemming from an earthquake epicentred near Sumatra, killed around a quarter of a million people. In 2005 Hurricane Katrina flooded New Orleans and an earthquake in Kashmir killed 80,000 people. In 2008 over 140,000 people were killed in Burma by a cyclone and nearly 70,000 in an earthquake in China. Just outside the noughties in 2011 a huge tsunami struck Japan, with over 25,000 feared dead.

In 2000, the Russian submarine Kursk sank, killing its crew of 118. The same year an Air France Concorde crashed killing all passengers. In 2003, the space shuttle, Columbia, blew up killing all seven astronauts onboard. Serbian PM Zoran Dindic was assassinated in 2003 as was Anna Lindh, Swedish foreign minister in the same year. Pakistan's former PM, Benazir Bhutto, was assassinated in 2007. In 2009 the world was warned of a swine flu pandemic; 12,000 died.

Email became the standard for written communications and the USB flash drive replaced the floppy disk for data storage. Windows XP and Microsoft Office 2003 became the norm for personal computer software (with subsequent updates). The online information source, Wikipedia, began in 2001 and became a reference standard. The Internet was increasingly used for buying anything and for downloading information. Google, Yahoo!, Amazon, eBay, Facebook, Twitter and YouTube all grew exponentially. Towards the end of the decade, high definition television became a reality. The sale of mobile phones grew, with many people having more than one. Laptops became smaller and the iPad was introduced and did phenomenally well. Skype took off as did eBooks. Most new cars were built with satellite navigation systems. Botox and cosmetic surgery in general became more fashionable and so did bottled water, the hybrid car, reusable shopping bags and online social networking.

In 2001 the world's first artificial heart was implanted. In 2006 a vaccine for cervical cancer was developed in Australia. Global warming and climate change continued to be a worldwide concern, but mostly in the West. Heatwaves, the increased number of hurricanes, melting ice and some rising sea levels all drew attention to the possible problem.

China became the economic powerhouse that economists predicted. Emerging economies in general (India and Brazil for example) grew in status, but the world's economy at large didn't. There was a credit crisis in much of the Western world in 2007 and several well-known banks and other financial organisations went to the wall. Others were saved by government intervention. The credit crunch, as it was called, led to a global financial crisis, the effects of which are still being felt. In 2008, Barack Obama became the first African-American president of the US. Michael Jackson died in 2009.

In popular literature, Harry Potter dominated along with Dan Brown's books, notably the terrific *The Da Vinci Code* (2003). Other rich literary veins included: *Speech! Speech!* (2000) by Geoffrey Hill, *The Blind Assassin* (2000) by Margaret Atwood, *The Tipping Point* (2000) by Malcolm Gladwell, *The Lovely Bones* (2002) by Alice Sebold, *Austerlitz (*2002) by W.G. Sebald and translated by Anthea Bell, *A Short History of Nearly Everything* (2003) by Bill Bryson, *Eats, Shoots and Leaves* (2003) by Lynne Truss, *The 2½ Pillars of Wisdom* (2004) by Alexander McCall Smith, *The Kite Runner* (2004) by Khaled Hosseini, *The Girl with the Dragon Tattoo* (2005) by Stieg Larsson and translated by Reg Keeland, *Never Let Me Go* (2005) by Kazuo Ishiguro, *Peeling the Onion* (2007) by Günter Grass and translated by Michael Henry Heim, *Harry Potter and the Deathly Hallows* (2007) by J.K. Rowling, *Descent into Chaos* (2008) by Ahmed Rashid and *Homicide* (2008) by David Simon.

In the theatre, there were some fascinating offerings, including: *Jesus Hopped The 'A' Train* (2000) by Stephen Adly Guirgis, *The Lieutenant of Inishmore* (2001) by Martin McDonagh, *The History Boys* (2004) by Alan Bennett and *ENRON* (2009) by Lucy Prebble.

In the world of film there were some major successes, including *X-Men*

(2000) and *X-Men 2* (2003), both directed by Bryan Singer, *X-Men: The Last Stand* (2006) directed by Brett Ratner, *Matrix Reloaded* (2003) and *The Matrix Revolutions* (also 2003) both written and directed by Larry and Andy Wachowski, *The Lord of the Rings* series directed by Peter Jackson, *Shrek* (2001) directed by Andrew Adamson and Vicky Jenson, *Shrek 2* (2004) directed by Andrew Adamson, Kelly Asbury and Conrad Vernon, *Spider Man* (2002) and *Spider Man 2* (2004), both directed by Sam Raimi, *Pirates of the Caribbean: The Curse of the Black Pearl* (2003), *Pirates of the Caribbean: Dead Man's Chest* (2006) and *Pirates of the Caribbean: At World's End* (2007), all directed by Gore Verbinski, *No Country for Old Men* (2007) directed by Joel and Ethan Coen, *Slumdog Millionaire* (2008) directed by Danny Boyle and *Avatar* (2009) directed by James Cameron.

There were a number of other inspirational films, including Ang Lee's *Crouching Tiger, Hidden Dragon* (2000), *Amélie* (2001) directed by Jean-Pierre Jeunet, *Spirited Away* (2001) directed by Hayao Miyazaki, *A Beautiful Mind* (2001) directed by Ron Howard, Baz Luhrmann's *Moulin Rouge!* (2001), Roman Polanski's *The Pianist* (2002), *Ice Age* (2002) directed by Carlos Saldanha and Chris Weddge, *City of God* (2002) directed by Fernando Meirelles and Kátia Lund, the Bourne triology: *The Bourne Identity* (2002) directed by Doug Liman, *The Bourne Supremacy* (2004) and *The Bourne Ultimatum* (2007), both directed by Paul Greengrass, Pixar's *Finding Nemo* (2003) directed by Lee Unkrich, *Lost in Translation* (2003) directed Sofia Coppola, *Cold Mountain* (2003) directed by Anthony Minghella, Clint Eastwood's *Letters from Iwo Jima* (2006), *Pan's Labyrinth* (2006) directed by Guillermo del Toro and Kathryn Biglow's *The Hurt Locker* (2009).

Other favourites would include: *Donnie Darko* (2001) directed by Richard Kelly, *Monsters, Inc.* (2001) by Pete Docter, and *Ratatouille* (2007) directed by Brad Bird. One of the films which set a tone and pace for the decade was *Gladiator* (2000) directed by Ridley Scott, so let's start with that.

From the film

86 GLADIATOR

directed by Ridley Scott (2000)

This film, set in Roman times, stars Russell Crowe who plays General Maximus Decimus Meridius, the eponymous gladiator. It won five Academy Awards, including Best Picture and Best Actor. The CGI in the film was largely experimental, but very successful. For example, Oliver Reed, who played slave manager Proximo, died during the film's shoot and CGI was used to map Reed's face onto a body double.

THE STORY

The emperor of Rome, Marcus Aurelius (Richard Harris), has a son Commudus (Joaquin Phoenix), who has few redeeming features and betrays Maximus (Russell Crowe), a loyal Roman general. Maximus is due to be given power to govern Rome by the emperor who believes his own son unfit to rule. Commudus murders his father and takes power. Maximus is stripped of his rank. His family is killed and he becomes a slave who ends up as a gladiator – eventually meeting the Emperor Commudus face-to-face and finally avenging the murder of his family and emperor. Maximus reinstates the Senate to govern Rome but, fatally wounded in the fight with Commudus, dies.

THE SPEECH

There is one now quite famous address at the beginning of the film when the then General Maximus pushes his men to fight and fight hard. The mix of humour and bravado inspires and comforts because we know we're on the side of heroes:

> “Fratres! Three weeks from now I will be harvesting my crops. Imagine where you will be and it will be so. Hold the line! Stay with me! If you find yourself alone, riding in green fields with the sun on your face, do not be troubled – for you are in Elysium, and you're already dead!”

Maximus means this as a joke, but not totally. The fact that he can have this close relationship with weary soldiers, many of whom are wounded, is indeed inspiring. There is another powerful moment, inspirational for different reasons. This is at the end of the film where Maximus at last faces his great enemy, Commudus:

> “Commudus: Rise. Rise. [Maximus stands]
>
> Commudus: Your fame is well deserved, Spaniard. I don't think there's ever been a gladiator to match you. As for this young man, he insists you are Hector reborn. Or was it Hercules? Why doesn't the hero reveal himself and tell us all your real name? You do have a name?
>
> Maximus: My name is Gladiator. [Maximus turns away]
>
> Commudus: How dare you show your back to me! Slave, you will remove your helmet and tell me your name.
>
> Maximus: [Removes helmet and turns around to face Commodus] My name is Maximus Decimus Meridius, commander of the Armies of the North, General of the Felix Legions, loyal servant to the true emperor, Marcus Aurelius. Father to a murdered son, husband to a murdered wife. And I will have my vengeance, in this life or the next. [Commudus stares in disbelief]”

From the film

87 BILLY ELLIOT

Directed by Stephen Daldry (2000)

This film starred Jamie Bell as Billy and is certainly sentimental, sometimes even verging on insincere. But there are times when the script, the acting and the scenarios work tremendously well to create an inspirational whole. It's set in the north of England during tough financial times in the mid-1980s. *Billy Elliot the Musical* was also a very successful show – with music by Elton John – and it's been doing well on both sides of the Atlantic since it hit the stage in 2005.

THE STORY

Eleven-year old Billy Elliot (Jamie Bell) misses his dead mother. His father Jackie (Gary Lewis) and older brother Tony (Jamie Draven) are striking coal miners. Also living with the family is Billy's grandmother (Jean Haywood) who, in her youth, also wanted to be a dancer.

To toughen Billy up, Jackie takes Billy to boxing classes. Billy hates boxing, but there are ballet lessons going on at the same sports' centre and Billy secretly begins to learn ballet, urged on by ballet teacher Georgia (Julie Walters). When Jackie discovers what's going on, he puts an end to this, but Georgia helps Billy in secret. She eventually thinks Billy has professional potential and wants him to apply to London's Royal Ballet School. Billy misses the audition though – due to the striking miners and Tony's arrest for fighting the police.

Georgia confronts Billy's father who is furious that his son is a burgeoning ballet dancer. But then Jackie sees Billy dance and realises his son indeed has talent. He raises the necessary money to take Billy to audition in London. Billy does well, but when teased by another (posh) boy, he thumps him. The audition board takes a dim view of this and Billy believes he's lost his one chance. However, all's well because he does get into the ballet school and becomes a successful dancer.

THE SPEECH

Humour very often pinpoints a moving moment. It's as old as storytelling itself and it's no less effective now:

> “Mrs. Wilkinson: This'll sound strange, Billy, but for some time now I've been thinkin' of the Royal Ballet School.
>
> Billy: Aren't you a bit old, miss?
>
> Mrs. Wilkisnon: No, not me ... you! I'm the bloody teacher!”

There are other times when pathos is used in exactly the same way as humour. Kind conversations helping the story along:

"Billy: I think I'm scared, Dad.

Dad: That's okay, son. We're all scared.

Billy: Well ... if I don't like it, can I still come back?

Dad: Are you kidding? We've let out your room [straight face, then laughter]."

FROM THE FILM

88 ERIN BROCKOVICH

DIRECTED BY STEVEN SODERBERGH (2000)

This film sees Julia Roberts playing Erin Brockovich, for which she won a Best Actress Oscar. Set in the US, it's about a real-life legal fight against a polluting energy company.

THE STORY

Lawyer Edward L. Mastry (Albert Finney) gives Erin Brockovich a job as a filing clerk in his legal practice. There she finds medical records concerning an energy company offering to purchase a particular home in a local town. Erin smells a rat and persuades Ed Mastry to allow her to dig further. She discovers that the company is quietly trying to buy land that was contaminated by a deadly toxic waste that has over time been illegally dumped, poisoning the local water supply and creating widespread illness amongst the area's residents. She learns of a huge cover-up.

Erin fights to bring the company to justice. Eventually, she gathers witnesses and evidence aware that, if she fails in her action, the results will be catastrophic. But she wins a great battle and we applaud as over six hundred people receive a sizeable settlement.

THE SPEECH

Here's a small piece of dialogue between Erin, Ed and the energy company's legal representatives, Ms Sanchez (Gina Gellego) and Mr. Walker (Don Snell):

"Ms Sanchez: Let's be honest here. Twenty million dollars is more money than these people have ever dreamed of.

Erin: Oh see, now that pisses me off. First of all … we have more than 400 plaintiffs and ... let's be honest, we all know there are more out there. They may not be the most sophisticated people, but they do know how to divide and twenty million dollars isn't shit when you split it between them. Second of all, these people don't dream about being rich. They dream about being able to watch their kids swim in a pool without worrying that they'll have to have a hysterectomy at the age of twenty. Like Rosa Diaz, a client of ours … So before you come back here with another lame ass offer, I want you to think real hard about what your spine is worth, Mr. Walker. Or what you might expect someone to pay you for your uterus, Ms Sanchez. Then you take out your calculator and you multiply that number by a hundred. Anything less than that is a waste of our time. [Ms Sanchez picks up a glass of water] By the way, we had that water brought in specially for you folks. Came from a well in Hinkley [where the contaminated water is].

Ms Sanchez: [Puts down the glass, without drinking] I think this meeting is over."

Again, we wish that we could manage moments like that.

FROM THE FILM

89 CAST AWAY

DIRECTED BY ROBERT ZEMECKIS (2000)

This isn't an easy to film to like. Not a lot happens in filmic terms and the story is one dimensional. However, Tom Hanks who stars as Chuck Noland, the protagonist, makes the film his own and the performance is strong. It's certainly uplifting.

THE STORY

FedEx employee Chuck Noland finds himself alone on the shores of a tropical island after a parcel delivery plane crash in the Pacific. He learns how to survive and he lives in hope that he'll see his fiancée Kelly again. It's this that keeps him going.

After what we imagine to have been four long years, Chuck manages to make a wooden raft and sets off across the ocean. He's rescued and finds it hard to settle back into civilization. He is shocked to find that Kelly is married with children. But it's not just loss and despair that affect him. It's adjusting to life as a whole. It's no longer the physical with which he has to cope, but also the seeking out of a new direction and, by the film's positive end, we believe that he will have found one.

THE SPEECH

There's a line in the film when Chuck has managed to get a raft together and is, at last, sailing away from the island. He doesn't know whether he can make it or not and he has no idea how far away he might be from land. But he has to try. Mr. Wilson is a volleyball and has become Chuck's only friend. Chuck gently puts the volleyball on the raft and says:

> “Don't worry Wilson, I'll do all the paddling. You just hang on.”

FROM THE FILM

90 A BEAUTIFUL MIND

DIRECTED BY RON HOWARD (2001)

This film, starring Russell Crowe, was based on the 1998 book of the same name by Sylvia Nasar. It won four Academy Awards. The true storyline is based on the life of John Forbes Nash, Jr., who was the 1994 Economics Noble Laureate.

THE STORY

Nash (Russell Crowe) is a mathematics whiz who has had mental health problems most of his life, even from his Princeton days. His ambition is to find a mathematical formula or theory that is unique. He keeps himself much to himself, his best and only real friend being his roommate Charles (Paul Bettany). Charles introduces him to his young niece, Marcee (Vivian Cardone) whom Nash comes to adore.

When Nash becomes an MIT professsor he meets graduate student Alicia (Jennifer Connolly) whom he marries. Nash becomes embroiled in work for the US government, primarily in code breaking, under the leadership of Willam Parcher (Ed Harris). Nash's paranoia stems partly from being chased and hunted by Russian agents. Over the next few years, Nash becomes so engrossed in himself and his work that he inhabits his own world and refuses to acknowledge the real one. He suffers from schizophrenia and is institutionalised. We discover that many of the people we have seen (Parcher, Charles, the Soviet agents) are his hallucinations. Gradually, he is reintroduced to society but he still imagines his friend Charles and Charles' niece Marcee. He teaches and again becomes involved in research and is much more at peace, despite the fact that his demons still trouble him from time to time.

THE SPEECH

Despite Nash's madness, or maybe because of it, he added value to science. He also inspired his wife and others to stand by him when he needed support. The film is about determination, overcoming great obstacles to succeed and perhaps most of all, passion. At the film's beginning we hear professor Helinger (Judd Hirsch) welcoming students, including Nash, to Princeton:

> “Mathematicians won the war. Mathematicians broke the Japanese codes ... and built the A-bomb. Mathematicians ... like you … In medicine or economics, in technology or space, battle lines are being drawn. To triumph, we need results. Publishable, applicable results. Now who among you will be the next Morse? The next Einstein? Who among you will be the vanguard of democracy, freedom, and discovery? … Welcome to Princeton, gentlemen.”

FROM THE FILM

91 THE PIANIST

DIRECTED BY ROMAN POLANSKI (2002)

This unsentimental film, based on the extraordinary events of Polish musician Wladyslaw Szpilman's life, starred Adrien Brody. It won three Oscars, including Best Actor and Best Director. The real Wladyslaw Szpilman died in 2000, aged 88, a few months before the film was made.

THE STORY

Wladyslaw Szpilman (Adrien Brody) watches as the civilised society of Warsaw is destroyed by the advancing Nazis. Szpilman relies on fortune and happenchance as his family and friends are humiliated, taken away to the ghetto and thereon to eventual annihilation in Treblinka. As his journey unfolds, we see that both sides have pure evil and angels. Through luck, he escapes the terrible tribulations suffered by other Jews. Through much of the film the music of Chopin features, except when Szpilman battles to stay alive with little food and no comfort. Later, he has to play for his life – literally – and is helped by a Nazi officer (Thomas Kretschmann). Szpilman survives.

THE SPEECH

A helpless Szpilman has no way to thank someone who has without question saved his life, apart from playing some piano. That the person is the enemy makes Szpilman (and, in a strange way, us) feel humble. And inspired:

“Szpilman: I don't know how to thank you.

Captain Wilm Hosenfeld: Thank God, not me. He wants us to survive. Well, that's what we have to believe.”

FROM THE FILM
92 BIG FISH
DIRECTED BY TIM BURTON (2003)

This film, based on a novel of the same name written by Daniel Wallace in 1998, is a heady mix of fairy tale and fantasy and is wonderfully warming. It targets the child inside any adult and doesn't insult our intelligence.

THE STORY

Edward Bloom (Albert Finney) is dying of cancer and his son, Will (Billy Crudup), is trying to learn more about his father's life. Will believes his father has lied throughout his life and never much cared for his family. As he lies dying, Edward takes his son and us on a tremendous journey through his life's many marvellous experiences, real or imagined. As Edward's story unfolds in flashback, Will tries to understand the truth about who his father really was. Each of Edward's stories has the look and feel of a fairy tale.

The younger Edward (Ewan McGregor) encounters many things throughout his life. He meets witches, giants and a werewolf and, on each occasion, he sees normality in a quirky world. As he is charmed, then so are we. However all these infectious experiences pale in comparison to the one thing in Edward's life that matters most – the search for his future wife Sandra (Alison Lohman, then Jessica Lange.)

THE SPEECH

We are inspired by the fantastic tales, each full of wonder and delight, that made Edward Bloom (literally). Whether or not they're true, we know that in Edward there is a positive man. Will sees this and is at last satisfied:

> “And telling the story of my father's life, it's impossible to separate fact from fiction, the man from the myth. The best I can do is to tell it the way he told me. It doesn't always make sense and most of it never happened ... but that's what kind of story this is.”

FROM THE FILM

93 LORD OF THE RINGS: RETURN OF THE KING

DIRECTED BY PETER JACKSON (2003)

This last of the Rings film trilogy contains superb acting and terrific effects. The music by Howard Shore is unforgettable and inspirational. The film won eleven Oscars.

THE STORY

To follow the plot fully, you'll really need to see the first two films or have read the book. Frodo (Elijah Wood) and Sam (Sean Astin), two hobbits, continue on their journey to the fires of Mount Doom where they can destroy the One Ring. Gollum (Andy Serkis), a former hobbit, corrupted by the power of the Ring, wants to lead them astray and to their doom; he plans to keep the Ring for himself.

Meanwhile, there is a great battle as the Evil Lord Sauron (Sala Baker) wages his last war against Middle-Earth. Sauron sets his sights on the kingdom of Gondor. According to legend, Gondor is to be ruled by a true king and we discover that the true king is to be Aragorn.

Eventually all ends well. The Ring is destroyed along with Gollum in the fires of Mount Doom, Sam and Frodo are rescued by eagles sent by the wizard Gandalf (Ian McKellen) and Aragorn (Viggo Mortenson) is pronounced King of the West. All the hobbits (the Fellowship) are safe.

THE SPEECH

Sam and Frodo are on what remains of Mount Doom, fearing that their end is nigh. Sam recollects life in the Shire, their home; the inspiration lies in the bond between the two:

“Sam: Do you remember the Shire, Mr. Frodo? It'll be spring soon. And the orchards will be in blossom. And the birds will be nesting in the hazel thicket. And they'll be sowing the summer barley in the lower fields

... and eating the first of the strawberries with cream. Do you remember the taste of strawberries?

Frodo: No, Sam. I can't recall the taste of food ... nor the sound of water ... nor the touch of grass. I'm ... naked in the dark, with nothing, no veil ... between me ... and the wheel of fire! I can see him... with my waking eyes!

Fredo: Then let us be rid of it ... once and for all! Come on, Mr. Frodo. I can't carry it for you ... but I can carry you!"

There's another moment – not a speech as such but extraordinarily inspiring. Towards the film's end on Mount Doom when the mountain is disintegrating, Gandalf, riding an eagle, saves Sam and Frodo. They wake up in Gondor, where they meet again the other hobbits who have shared the big adventure. Aragorn is crowned King of Gondor. After the wedding of Aragorn and his true love Arwen (Liv Tyler), the four hobbits bow to Aragorn. But Aragorn says,

> "My friends. You bow to no one."

It is he who kneels and the entire kingdom follows suit, kneeling to the hobbits. It is a great moment and is hugely inspirational: the humility, the gentleness, the quiet after the raging wars, a kind of closure.

FROM THE FILM

94 LOVE ACTUALLY

DIRECTED BY RICHARD CURTIS (2003)

Starring Hugh Grant, this is a romantic, heartwarming, fun and cheery film that's pure cosy entertainment. It shows us ten stories, each in its own way inspirational and, as each unfolds, the stories and their characters mingle.

THE STORY

It's London and five weeks before Christmas. David (Hugh Grant) has just become the UK's new prime minister. He falls for Natalie, one of his staff. David's sister Karen (Emma Thompson), married to Harry (Alan Rickman), begins to realise that all's not well with their relationship. Harry, who runs a magazine, has his eye on his secretary Mia (Heike Makatsch) and she flirts with him. Sarah (Laura Linney), one of the magazine's editors, has a brother in a care home whom she adores. Sarah likes Karl (Rodrigo Santoro) and that's reciprocated, but Sarah's brother comes first and therefore the relationship between Sarah and Karl is only taking off very slowly. Karen has a close friend in Daniel (Liam Neeson), a recent widower with a young stepson who has a crush on a young American girl from school. John (Martin Freeman) and Judy (Joanna Page) are pornographic film stand-ins who grow closer after their simulated love scenes.

Then there's Jamie (Colin Firth), a writer whose girlfriend has just left him for his younger brother. Jamie moves to France to finish his novel and there falls for a beautiful Portuguese woman, Aurélia (Lúcia Moniz), whose lack of English matches Jamie's lack of Portuguese. Juliet (Keira Knightley) has just married Peter (Chiwetel Ejiofor), but his best buddy Mark (Andrew Lincoln) secretly adores Juliet. Another character, Colin (Kris Marshall), wants lots of sex and so heads off to the US, believing that women will fall for him because he's British. Then there's Billy Mack (Bill Nighy), an ageing rock star fighting a drug addiction who suddenly has a hit song on his hands: *Love is All Around.* In the end, nearly everyone more or less ends up happily ever after. Great entertainment and life affirming.

THE SPEECH

The British prime minister's voice-over prologue – as the credits run – is delivered with shots of arrivals at London's Heathrow Airport. We see all sorts of people greeting their loved ones. It makes us a smile.

“Whenever I get gloomy with the state of the world, I think about the arrivals gate at Heathrow Airport. General opinion's starting to make out that we live in a world of hatred and greed, but I don't see that. It seems to me that love is everywhere. Often it's not particularly dignified or newsworthy, but it's always there … if you look for it, I've got a sneaky feeling you'll find that love actually is all around.”

FROM THE PLAY

95 THE HISTORY BOYS

DIRECTED BY NICHOLAS HYTNER (2004)

This play by Alan Bennett was made into a film in 2006 by Hytner, who also directed the original production of the play in London. The play was very well received both in UK and America.

THE STORY

Set in the 1980s, the play focuses on eight boys at a small public school in Yorkshire, England: their education, philosophies, general sexual and moral awareness. This awareness is helped along by two teachers who are poles apart in attitude and approach.

Hector, a General Studies teacher, loves literature and willingly shares his knowledge. He is confident and his teaching is engaging The school's two-faced headmaster cares only for league tables and propriety. He recruits another teacher, Irwin, to coach history to prepare the boys for their Oxford and Cambridge University entrance exams. However, Irwin is not a golden teacher either and twists history to make it suit his own views.

Hector occasionally gives the boys rides home on his motorbike and fondles his charges. The boys laugh this off, but Hector is reported on one occasion and is asked to retire. Until he does, the headmaster also insists that Hector and Irwin share a class. All the boys get to Oxford or Cambridge.

Hector dies in a motorbike accident while giving Irwin a ride. Irwin suffers severe injuries and memory loss and is now wheelchair-bound. We discover, at the end of the play, what has become of the boys in later life. It's a moving moment. None of the boys have achieved their full potential and all are in some way disillusioned. Irwin has given up teaching and now makes TV documentaries.

THE SPEECH

We all remember at least one teacher who inspired us at some point in our education. Here Hector says:

> "The best moments in reading are when you come across something – a thought, a feeling, a way of looking at things – that you'd thought special, particular to you. And here it is, set down by someone else, a person you've never met, maybe even someone long dead. And it's as if a hand has come out and taken yours."

Beautifully written and a beautifully put sentiment.

FROM THE FILM

96 SPIDER-MAN 2

DIRECTED BY SAM RAIMI (2004)

This film starred Tobey McGuire and won an Academy Award. It certainly reinforced in kids of a certain age that being Spider-Man must be the best thing ever.

THE STORY

Peter Parker (Tobey McGuire) finds life tough. Being Spider-Man has brought him nothing but headaches as far as his personal life is concerned. Worse, the love of his life, Mary Jane Watson (Kirsten Dunst) has become engaged to another, John Jameson (Daniel Gillies), an astronaut. Peter decides that he doesn't want to be a superhero any more, until a new danger appears in the form of Dr Otto Octavius (Alfred Molina), also known as Dr Octopus, a super-villain with four metal tentacles protruding from his body.

Peter realises that only Spider-Man can stop him but, of course, that's not going to be a straightforward operation. Mary Jane gets caught in the middle which only complicates matters and Harry Osborn (James Franco) still blames Spider-Man for the death of his father, Norman Osborn

(Wilem Dafoe), who was also the Green Goblin. Harry wants Spider-Man dead. Eventually, Osborn finds out who Spider-Man is, horrified that it's his best friend, Peter. Octavius regains his sanity and saves the city from destruction, sacrificing his own life in the process. Mary Jane doesn't marry her astronaut – she wants Peter instead, although she knows he will always be Spider-Man first.

THE SPEECH

Peter is depressed about the loss of his girlfriend and the schism between himself and his friend Harry. He wants to give up fighting crime. His Aunt May (Rosemary Harris) reminds him that their neighbour, young Henry (Jason Fiore-Ortiz), is sad that Spider-Man has all but disappeared. She gives him this inspirational advice and we know she knows Peter's secret:

> "He [Henry] knows a hero when he sees one. Too few characters out there, flying around like that, saving old girls like me. And Lord knows, kids like Henry need a hero. Courageous, self-sacrificing people setting examples for all of us … I believe there's a hero in all of us that keeps us honest, gives us strength, makes us noble and finally allows us to die with pride … Spider-Man did that for Henry and he wonders where he's gone. He needs him."

FROM THE FILM

97 PAN'S LABYRINTH

DIRECTED BY GUILLERMO DEL TORO (2006)

This film, also written by del Toro, is beautifully made and won three Oscars. It's a dark fairy tale that mixes fact and fantasy, delight and hurt.

THE STORY

It's 1944 and the Spanish Civil War has ended, but rebels still fight in the mountains against the fascist troops. Young Ofelia (Ivana Baquero) goes with her pregnant and sick mother, Carmen Vidal (Ariadna Gil), to the country to live in an ancient mill house with her stepfather, the cruel Captain Vidal (Sergi López i Ayats). One night, Ofelia sees a fairy and together they go to the centre of a maze where they meet a strange magical creature – a faun – who tells her that she's a princess from a kingdom in the underground. He also tells that her (real) father – the King of the Underworld – is waiting for her, but she needs to accomplish three dangerous tasks first before she can see him.

Meanwhile, Ofelia becomes friendly with household servant Mercedes (Maribel Verdú), the sister of one of the rebels, who is giving tacit help to the rebel group. Ofelia tries to complete her tasks that will guarantee her immortality and the chance of seeing her father again. The film ends with the death of both the cruel stepfather and Ofelia. We really aren't certain whether she is indeed dead or in the magical realm.

THE SPEECH

There are times when innocence expressed in words, music, art, film or theatre can be all-pervading. At the end of this film we hear Pan say:

> "And it is said that the Princess returned to her father's kingdom. That she reigned there with justice and a kind heart for many centuries. That she was loved by her people. And that she left behind small traces of her time on Earth, visible only to those who know where to look."

We ache to make it so.

From the film

98 RATATOUILLE

Directed by Brad Bird (2007)

This animated film produced by Pixar won an Academy Award for Best Animated Feature.

THE STORY

Remy is a gourmet rat with a keen smell, fascinated by gourmet cooking. He gets into the kitchen of the house where he and his rat family lives to read the cookery book of his absolute hero – Parisian chef Auguste Gusteau. Gusteau's mantra is that anyone can cook. Remy discovers that Gusteau has just died following a terrible review from nasty, mean and world-hating food critic Anton Ego (Peter O'Toole).

Remy arrives in Paris and finds Gusteau's old restaurant now run by Gusteau's former sous chef, Skinner (Ian Holm). Alfredo Linguini, a feckless youth, who is actually Gusteau's son, works at the restaurant as a cleaner. When he spills a pot of soup, he tries to make a new batch but hasn't a clue how. Remy, seeing this, tries to put the soup right by adding the correct ingredients. Linguini sees Remy; Skinner catches Linguini. But the soup tastes terrific and another chef, Colette, persuades Skinner to be lenient. But Linguini has to make the soup again and needs Remy to help. Remy sits under Linguini's chef's hat directing the boy to put in the right ingredients.

Skinner discovers Linguini's parentage but won't tell the youth for fear of losing the restaurant to Linguini. The plot thickens, not least with Linguini and Colette falling in love.

Eventually Linguini, Colette and Remy set up a new restaurant called Ratatouille, which successfully caters for rats and people separately.

THE SPEECH

We always like it when a bad person becomes good. Here, food critic Anton Ego who, up to now, has been gravelly and ghastly to everyone, eats the wonderful ratatouille at Gusteau's restaurant and then writes this inspirational review:

"… The world is often unkind to new talent, new creations. The new needs friends. Last night, I experienced something new, an extraordinary meal from a singularly unexpected source. To say that both the meal and its maker have challenged my preconceptions about fine cooking is a gross understatement. They have rocked me to my core … It is difficult to imagine more humble origins than those of the genius now cooking at Gusteau's, who is, in this critic's opinion, nothing less than the finest chef in France. I will be returning to Gusteau's soon, hungry for more.”

FROM THE FILM

99 SLUMDOG MILLIONAIRE

DIRECTED BY DANNY BOYLE (AND IN INDIA BY LOVELEEN TANDAN) (2008)

This film, adapted from novel *Q & A,* published in 2005 by Vikas Swarup, won eight Academy Awards including Best Picture and Best Director. It is an inspirational, feel-good film.

THE STORY

Jamal Malik (Dev Patel), an eighteen year-old orphan from the slums of Mumbai, is just one single question away from winning twenty million rupees in the Indian version of the TV quiz show, *Who Wants to be a Millionaire?* However, during an overnight break in the programme's production, Jamal is arrested under the suspicion of cheating. People don't believe that a young man his age could be so knowledgeable.

To prove his innocence, Jamal tells his life story in a series of flashbacks. We are taken to the slums where he grew up with his brother, Salim (Madhur Mittal), and where the two of them stole to exist and had battles with thugs to survive. We also meet Latika (Freida Pinto), the girl he loved. Each part of his story shows how he knows the answers to each of the quiz show's questions. We learn that Salim has become a top thug in a criminal gang. Latika, we discover, has been held captive by Salim. The only way Jamal can think of to getting her to see him is via *Who Wants to be a Millionaire?,* which Jamal knows Latika watches avidly.

Jamal gets through to the final question even though the show's sneering host Prem Kumar (Anil Kapoor) is unpleasant. Back at the police station, the police inspector (Irrfan Khan) believes Jamal, who is then allowed to complete the quiz. Meanwhile, Latika is watching what's happening to Jamal on TV at the gangsters' hideout. Salim wants to make amends and lets Latika go.

Jamal gets the answer to the last question right by sheer guesswork, but he's happy knowing that Latika is well and safe. The film ends with our happy couple singing and dancing on a railway platform.

THE SPEECH

The whole film is a story of inspiration – there are small, touching moments where, with a little dialogue, we understand that eventually all will be well:

> "Latika: You want to do something for me?
>
> Jamal: Anything.
>
> Latika: Then forget me!"

Another moment is one of tension – we know that Jamal will play on in the quiz and we admire the simplicity and courage of both perseverance and faith:

> "Prem Kumar: Final question for twenty million rupees, and he's smiling. I guess you know the answer.
>
> Jamal: Do you believe it, I don't.
>
> Prem Kumar: You don't? So you take the ten million and walk?
>
> Jamal: No. I'll play."

One more moment worthy of your patience:

> "Police inspector [whispering]: Doctors ... lawyers ... never get past sixty thousand rupees. He's won ten million. [pause] What the hell can a slumdog possibly know?
>
> Jamal Malik [quietly]: The answers. [spits out blood, then says quietly and gently] I knew the answers."

From the film

100 AVATAR

Directed by James Cameron (2009)

This film broke box office records and became the highest-grossing film of all time in the US. It also went on to break records worldwide and three Oscars. There is an Avatar triology planned.

THE STORY

The film is set in 2154. Humans are mining a precious mineral called Unobtanium on a moon called Pandora that could solve the ecological crisis on Earth. Unfortunately, the mining of this precious mineral threatens the life and very existence of the local inhabitants – the Na'Vi tribe. Paraplegic Marine Jake Sully (Sam Worthington) decides to take his place in a mission to Pandora. He discovers there is a plan to get rid of the Na'Vi so that the mineral can be mined at will, destroying the planet. In a bargain that will give him surgery so as to walk again, Jake adopts an avatar character and infiltrates the Na'Vi tribe. Jake eventually becomes friendly with the tribe and falls for the beautiful Neytiri (Zoe Saldana). He starts to see the world through the tribe's eyes and realises how much the Na'vi tribe means to him. He decides he wants to help, thereby risking his real and avatar lives. Eventually, the corporation is beaten and Jake becomes a permanent avatar.

THE SPEECH

The film is extraordinary on many levels – the merging of real life action with animation, the introduction of 3D that doesn't make your eyes uncomfortable and allows you to see depth when it matters. It is strictly a traditional good versus evil storyline and Colonel Quaritch (Stephen Lang) is the epitome of the tough, bad guy whose job it is to lead the mining corporation to military success. To Jake, when the marine becomes slightly suspect, Colonel Quaritch says:

"You haven't got lost in the woods, have you? You still remember what team you're playing for?"

In briefing his team, the Colonel paints a picture of doom and gloom. Funnily enough, it is he who's recalled long after the film ends.

"You are not in Kansas anymore. You are on Pandora, ladies and gentlemen. Respect that fact every second of every day. If there is a Hell, you might want to go there for some R & R after a tour on Pandora. Out there beyond that fence every living thing that crawls, flies, or squats in the mud wants to kill you and eat your eyes for jujubes. We have an indigenous population of humanoids called the Na'vi. They're fond of arrows dipped in a neurotoxin that will stop your heart in one minute – and they have bones reinforced with naturally occurring carbon fibre. They are very hard to kill. As head of security, it is my job to keep you alive. I will not succeed. Not with all of you. If you wish to survive, you need to cultivate a strong, mental aptitude. You got to obey the rules: Pandora rules. Rule number one ..."

AN OVERVIEW OF CHAPTER EIGHT

To be entertained is always a reason for going to the cinema or theatre – maybe it's *the* reason. But I also think that it has something to do with discovering more about oneself. That's enjoyable and sometimes surprising, particularly when a piece holds up a mirror to oneself. But learning about oneself and ways of mankind can also be fraught. In *Cast Away* we have a powerful character study of a man and his quest for physical and mental survival. We're drawn into his long, arduous journey as he struggles not only to keep his sanity, but to stay alive so he can make it back to the love of his life. In the film *Big Fish,* the questing son at one point remarks to his bedridden father that he's heard all of his stories thousands of times, and he has no idea who his father really is. The father's reply is, "I've never been anybody but me from the day I was born. If you don't know who I am, that's your failing, not mine." One didn't need a surprise ending or secret identities to make this film enjoyable. Ed Bloom shows us how exaggerations and erroneous behaviour are an integral part of our lives. *Big Fish* becomes a melting pot of proclivities establishing a rich obituary for anyone.

The History Boys reaffirms our joy of language and argument, of inspirational teachers, mentors and literature. *Love Actually* is a fun romp with a tale that allows us to feel comfortable and that too is important from time to time. Good versus evil is the perennial story and is epitomised in the escapism of *Spider-Man* and, in a very different way in *Pan's Labyrinth*, which is as powerful and inspirational as any deep-rooted story from the worlds of Shakespeare or Dickens. *Slumdog Millionaire* allows us the anticipation of good and decency winning over corruption. We know how the end will work out but we of course enjoy the roller-coaster ride that gets us there, on the journey inspired by characters and emotion. And *Avatar*, again extolling good over bad, is a visual feast as well as a story well told.

Lord of the Rings: Return of the King is a fairytale without any ambition other than to tell us a story of good versus evil. The whole narrative maintains our interest and spirit and that is, as we now well know, the purpose of an inspirational story!

CONCLUSION

"… This story shall the good man teach his son." From The St Crispin Day speech in *Henry V* by William Shakespeare

"There is a story in the Talmud about a king who had a son who went astray. The son was told, 'Return to your father.' The son replied that he could not. The king then sent a messenger to the son with the message 'Come back to me as far as you can, and I will meet you the rest of the way.'" Barry Miller as Reuven from the film *The Chosen* (1981)

Well, there's not a great deal to add really. That herewith are my special moments is a selfish notion, but I suspect there are some with which you will agree. Each has the propensity to make me weep, smile or grin hugely. Inspiration does that. It is of course a shame that I cannot continue with another one hundred moments here, including films and plays from 2011. Already I like the idea of films such as *The King's Speech* (directed by Tom Hooper), *True Grit* (directed by the Coen brothers), *Le Quattro Volte* (directed by Michelangelo Frammartino), *Contagion* (directed by Steven Soderbergh) and *Unknown White Male* (directed by Jaume Collet-Serra). But I also like the idea of including inspiration from the likes of Shakespeare, Jonson, Webster, Marlowe, Dryden, Congreve, Wilde, Ibsen, Shaw, Chekov, Albee, O'Neill, Brecht, Osborne, Orton, Stoppard and Frayn – amongst many others. Maybe that'll happen.

In *The Spectator* magazine (October 2010), actor Kevin Spacey, director of the Old Vic, wrote an article about public funding for the arts. He maintained that we need to be inspired by our arts, that we need to be refreshed culturally, whatever that may mean to each of us. Spacey says that we're "all eager for moments of inspiration". Most of the time, being inspired does us a world of good. As Clarence the angel in the film *It's a Wonderful Life* (1946) says, "Strange, isn't it? Each man's life touches so many other lives. When he isn't around he leaves an awful hole, doesn't he?"

ABOUT THE AUTHOR

Simon Maier has been involved in delivering events for 23 years throughout the world and for every imaginable purpose. In the mid-1980s he led much of the event activity in the UK for the privatization of several blue chip companies, and has ever since been responsible for a wide variety of corporate and public events.

As its managing director, Simon led Saatchi-owned ICM to record turnover and profit levels and then did much the same for a number of other leading event and experiential businesses, including his own.

He is frequently invited to comment on what makes a great speech and a speaker great, in the course of which he explains how people can have the first and become the second. Simon is also in demand as a conference facilitator, in which role many CEOs regard him as an event playmaker or quarterback. Despite that, he can't play American football. But he can be contacted on simonmaier@btinternet.com.